# MARKETING AT LOW TIDE

## HOW TO RECESSION-PROOF
## YOUR MARKETING DEPARTMENT

by

Allison Tivnon

GoNoGo Consulting

Portland, Oregon

Published by GoNoGo Consulting

ISBN 978-1-7357437-0-7

Library of Congress Control Number: 2020917446

Printed in the United States of America
Set in Georgia & Brandon Grotesque fonts
Cover Designed by Brandi Doane McCann
Graphic Elements by Tina Morgan
Illustrations by Eric Wimberly
Edited by Laura Knudson

*For Laura Knudson, Emmy Haveman, and Adam Lopez*

# ACKNOWLEDGMENTS

This book would not have been possible without the support and feedback of my fellow marketing professionals. Each of the following individuals graciously dedicated their time to a series of interviews—sharing their journeys, vulnerabilities, and insights.

Jewel Bergeron | Christina Blaser | Tanya Boyer
Angie Cole | Melissa Crosman | Paul Dickow | Lindsay Dunton
Gregory Fritz | Connie Gilfillan | Kelly Johnson
Frank Lippert, FSMPS, CPSM | Damion Morris, CPSM
Cheryl Nervez | Kelsey Parpart, CPSM | Katherine Pokrass
Michael Reilly, FSMPS | McKenzie Richardson
Craig Runyon | Christopher Tejeda, CPSM | Bonnie Temple, CPSM

Thank you to the Society for Marketing Professional Services. SMPS has played a pivotal role in my career since I entered the A/E/C industry in 2008—in both the high and low tides.

And last but not least, thank you to my husband Eric and son Jack. I love you guys 3,000.

"A recession can be a blessing ... as it is much easier to spot a strong company without the noise of a strong economy."

*Industries that Thrive on Recession*
THE DENVER POST

# TABLE OF CONTENTS

Introduction         i

**Section I: Recession and the A/E/C Industry**    1

**Chapter 1** Remembering '08 in the A/E/C Industry    3

**Chapter 2** Why Firms Cut Marketing Resources    7

**Chapter 3** How Marketing Can Change Firm Psychology    15

**Chapter 4** We're in a Recession, Now What?    25

**Section II: Four Recession Action Steps**    29

**Chapter 5** Recession Response #1
The 'Check-Up' Checklist Assessment    31

**Chapter 6** Recession Response #2
Staff Assessment and Cross Training    35

**Chapter 7** Recession Response #3
Historical Analysis of the Great Recession    43

**Chapter 8** Recession Response #4
Marketing Report-Backs    47

## Section III: Ten Essential Annual Tasks   51

**Chapter 9**  Know Your Flow: Calculating Proposal Peaks   53

**Chapter 10**  Creating Your Annual Marketing Calendar   59

**Chapter 11**  It Takes a Village: Dialing in Staff Roles and Responsibilities   63

**Chapter 12**  The Critical Value of Interns   71

**Chapter 13**  Tighten Up Leads Tracking   75

**Chapter 14**  The Client Survey   79

**Chapter 15**  Digital Marketing: Reach Your Audience Without Wasting Your Time   85

**Chapter 16**  Establish (or Refine) Your Marketing Budget   89

**Chapter 17**  Create Transparency in Your Marketing Tasks   93

**Chapter 18**  Retreat!   97

## Section IV: Caught in the Undertow
## What Comes After a Layoff   111

**Chapter 19**  Looking Out at the Horizon   113

# MARKETING AT LOW TIDE

If you're reading this, you have likely found yourself in the midst of a significant transition within your firm—from an economic expansion to one of contraction. Where the ground beneath your feet may have felt solid, it now feels more like sand. You're looking for guideposts and a compass to help chart your marketing activities in an economy rife with uncertainty. As your company absorbs the impacts of this new economic climate, all eyes are on marketing. How are we going to respond? How are we going to shift our resources? You may even feel unease in your job security as your firm weighs the cost and value of 'overhead' expenses.

This book is meant to center your thoughts around the tactics needed to re-orient your mind and marketing resources. The wear and tear of a strong economic expansion can take a toll on our marketing operations and make it difficult to pivot into recession. Any stumbles in our agility send signals to our firm leadership that we may not be up to the task of weathering an economic downturn.

To prevent this from happening, it is important to take a step back and reflect—to both understand the motivations and perceptions that drive firm financial decisions, as well as to clinically review our marketing operations.

This book provides an overview of the impacts of recession on the A/E/C industry and explores the firm psychology that drives decisions that affect marketing and business development staff. Once we have a broader context for these forces, we can plan for and respond to them using a series of actionable steps.

On the surface, a recession may not seem like a blessing. But it can serve as an opportunity to shore up your team's operations and reinforce your value to your firm's leadership.

We react in expansions. We proact in recessions.

Let's get proactive.

# RECESSION AND THE
# A/E/C INDUSTRY

"Just like the Great Depression shaped the way our grandparents viewed and spent money,
I think the Great Recession of '08 shaped the way A/E/C firms make decisions and
investments. There were a lot of lessons learned about where to make cuts."
Gregory F. (Marketing and Business Development Manager,
engineering/environmental firm)

To know where we're going, we have to know where we've been. While many marketing professionals were in the business during the last recession, many were still in college at the time. Some were still in high school! For those who are experiencing a recession for the first time while on the job, you may be wondering 'What exactly are we in for?" For those who have been through this before you may be wondering "Will this be like last time?"

It's important to pause and reflect—to understand the mechanics of a recession and how it impacts the A/E/C industry, as well as our marketing departments. We must understand the psychology that drives firm financial decisions and why this often has negative repercussions for marketing professionals. We work in a distinctly niche corner of the marketing world—one that is 'homegrown' in many ways. The textbook rules of marketing often only loosely apply to us, and our value and identity is often driven by the unique characteristics and idiosyncrasies of our firms. To prevent a 'devaluation' of marketing in times of recession, we need to begin by rooting ourselves in why it happens in the first place.

# CHAPTER ONE

# REMEMBERING '08
# IN THE A/E/C INDUSTRY

*"I experienced a layoff during the recession. I was working in one of the largest mechanical engineering firms in the country, managing a marketing team of five. We did a lot of work in the housing industry. We grew really fast during this time and didn't have infrastructure in place to deal with economic downturns…. We peaked at 1,700, almost 1,800, employees and fell below 300 by the time it was over."*
Christopher T. (Marketing and Business Development Manager, engineering firm, speaking about a former employer)

For many professionals in the A/E/C industry, 2008 doesn't seem that long ago. The effects of the Great Recession impacted virtually all facets of everyday life. While that particular recession was triggered by the financial sector, housing speculation, and disastrous lending practices, the impacts upended stability across most market sectors and had crippling effects on spending and tax revenue. As private-sector growth stalled and government agencies collected less in taxes, private and public work projects slowed and A/E/C firms in turn saw their pipelines shrink to unprofitable levels.

This reduction in incoming work was immediate for some and delayed for others. Construction firms, for instance, experienced the impacts almost from the start as stop-work orders went into effect and funding was rescinded. Cranes began disappearing from the skyline and half-finished buildings became a symbol for an industry brought to a standstill. Engineering and architecture firms were next as subsequent phases of ongoing projects were put on hold indefinitely and new projects canceled or delayed. Planning firms typically experienced the greatest lag time, as these projects—lower in cost—were often carried out, but with a significant decrease in new planning projects as government agencies took a step back to balance their budgets and reevaluate funding priorities.

Up until the recession hit, many A/E/C firms were enjoying healthy profit margins and strong growth across service sectors. In the 'good times', firms naturally look for ways to maximize profits, which can include geographic market expansions, office build-outs, new service offerings, and investments in technology and innovation. This is true of most business models. It is also true that, depending on the timing of these investments, firms that made big financial commitments close to when the recession began were left in dire financial predicaments—with too much capital leveraged and dwindling profits to cover their investments.

Due to these factors, layoffs swept through the A/E/C industry. Firms shrank in size and many notable mergers and acquisitions occurred. Many firms found themselves at the break-even point or even in 'the red', with growing lines of credit and accumulated debt. Cost-cutting measures naturally followed and firm leadership began putting all company spending under a microscope—evaluating where the money was going and determining what was and wasn't 'essential' to the company's survival. As a result, A/E/C marketing staff experienced enormous impacts as firms downsized, shuttered, or merged with other firms. Many of these professionals—particularly in senior management positions—were laid off in an effort to cut costs.

"In the Great Recession, people were getting laid off and not getting re-hired because there were no jobs. And the jobs that did come up didn't pay as well. Many firms laid off their Marketing Managers and Directors and they didn't necessarily rehire for those roles. They would hire coordinators instead because they cost less. A lot of senior-level staff found themselves having to start over." – Tanya B. (Marketing Manager, engineering firm)

In an article entitled "Quantifying the Impact of the Great Recession on the A/E/C Industry—A Call to Reevaluate Home Office Overhead Costs" for the *International Journal of Construction Education and Research*, a survey of 437 construction firms was conducted. The survey was meant to identify trends in cost-cutting strategies throughout the industry. The survey offered numerous categories of overhead expenses (including business development) and as the data suggests in the following table, the vast majority of firms employed cost reductions across the board.

Table 1. Descriptive Statistics for Overhead-Reduction Categories

| Overhead Category | # of responses | Mean | Median | Mode | Standard deviation |
|---|---|---|---|---|---|
| Bonuses | 425 | 2.233 | 2 | 0 | 1.940 |
| Company functions (parties, etc.) | 410 | 2.239 | 2 | 0 | 1.833 |
| Charitable and holiday gifts | 426 | 1.988 | 2 | 0 | 1.703 |
| Training and education | 432 | 1.021 | 0 | 0 | 1.412 |
| Contributions to retirement plans | 424 | 1.297 | 0 | 0 | 1.853 |
| Corporate officer salary | 418 | 1.077 | 0 | 0 | 1.367 |
| Business development and accounting staff | 429 | 0.854 | 0 | 0 | 1.375 |
| Travel and company vehicles | 425 | 1.228 | 1 | 0 | 1.438 |
| Home office: space (i.e., rent) | 408 | 0.398 | 0 | 0 | 0.919 |
| Home office: benefits paid by company | 400 | 0.511 | 0 | 0 | 1.051 |
| Home office: number of hours worked | 402 | 0.359 | 0 | 0 | 0.879 |
| Home office: staff salary | 403 | 0.492 | 0 | 0 | 0.957 |
| Home office: insurance costs | 392 | 0.450 | 0 | 0 | 0.962 |
| **Other descriptive statistics** | | | | | |
| Number of overhead categories reduced | 437 | 5.524 | 5 | 6 | 3.421 |

"Quantifying the Impact of the Great Recession on the A/E/C Industry—A Call to Reevaluate Home Office Overhead Costs", Jake B. Smithwick, Thomas C. Schleifer, et al, International Journal of Construction Education and Research, July 3, 2019, Taylor & Francis.
Reprinted by permission of the publisher (Taylor & Francis ltd, http://www.tandfonline.com)

While these 'company-saving' efforts are necessary, it can—and should—be argued that marketing staff should be evaluated outside of the 'overhead' category. Marketing is, by definition, an investment that a firm makes in an effort to bring in new work. The nature of the job is to increase revenue. By removing staff whose sole purpose is to build brand awareness and secure new work, companies increase their likelihood of remaining unprofitable *longer* than firms that position themselves for when their market sectors begin to recover. Indeed, in other industries, such as consumer goods and manufacturing, the business doctrine enshrines marketing and business development into every strategic conversation and investment decision. To cut in this area, means not only a decrease in market share, but also long-term impacts to future growth as competitors gain field advantage.

"The impact on the firm I was working at was immediate. There was a 5-person marketing department and by the time it was over, I was the only one left. When my Marketing Director left, I had to take on her workload as well as the work of the other coordinators but without any change in my salary." – Kelly J. (Marketing Director, civil engineering and planning firm, speaking about a former employer)

---

**The Great Recession (December 2007–June 2009)**

Housing markets collapsed and new construction ground to a halt

Major financial institutions failed and the stock markets plunged

Household debt rose dramatically, spending slowed significantly

Massive layoffs occurred in the industry trades and manufacturing

Millions of homes went into foreclosure

Tax bases shrunk

**Public and private sector growth stalled**

RFPs slowed to a trickle

Contracts were canceled

On-calls stopped producing new work

Public agencies started keeping as much work in-house as possible

**A/E/C firms felt the effect and began cost-saving measures**

---

# CHAPTER TWO

# WHY FIRMS CUT MARKETING RESOURCES

"They thought they could shift marketing work to administrative staff and achieve the same results." – Cheryl N. (Business Development Manager, architecture firm, speaking about a former employer)

Given the tendency to make deep—and often shortsighted—cuts in marketing and business development staff, the question naturally is: Why?

Why would firms in a competitive B2B industry sacrifice their business development staff? Why would firms eliminate the very positions dedicated to ensuring brand strength in an increasingly competitive environment?

The answer is: because most firms forget that they are a **brand** first and a **service provider** second.

Most of our firms were founded by smart, successful consultants who achieved their success based on their personal reputation for doing good work. Indeed, many of our firms are named after them. The marketing culture of these companies is often shaped by a belief that personal brand development of technical staff is the key to differentiating a firm from the competition—that the quality of service alone will distinguish the firm from others.

This is simply not true.

While quality of service is critically important, most—*if not all*—firms tout the quality of the work they perform. The truth is, while our companies may have been named after a founder, most of these founders have long since retired and handed the reigns over to successors. What remains is the *spirit* of what that founder brought to the competitive field—their ideals that inspired others to come work for the company, that led to logo creation and taglines, a color palette and 'look and feel' of the company website and work products. What is left is a *brand*. And that brand must be nurtured and enhanced if it is to survive.

And while a brand is only as good as the services rendered, once you have attained 'brand status' you *must* have marketing professionals there to protect and support it.

But the fact is, the vast majority of firms in the A/E/C industry are small. According to the 2010 census, most firms employ less than 20 people.[1] Small and mid-size firms are typically not run by MBAs or professionals trained specifically in business operations. They are run by the very people who provide the services.

Architects run architecture firms, engineers run engineering firms, and so on.

"There is a perception in the A/E/C industry that marketing is a 'nice-to-have' not a 'need-to-have'. In most smaller firms marketing grew out of the administrative space and the 'old guard' owners of these firms just don't recognize that there are underlying skills and talents to marketing and communication that exist outside their frame of reference."
Damion M. (Proposal Manager, construction firm)

When 'seller/doers' are at the very top of the leadership pyramid, there is a tendency to place an out-sized emphasis on the work itself and on the personal 'brands' of the top project directors or principals. This reliance on personal brand development nurtures a misconception that, as a firm grows in size, the brand will continue to grow based solely on the work product and

[1] "Mind-Blowing Stats from the Census Bureau", *Engineering News-Record*, October 14, 2014.

reputations of the technical staff. They tend to view marketers as 'fulfillment' staff—employed merely to service the needs of technical staff as they pursue new work. Track the leads, coordinate the proposals, staff the booth, maintain the website, and so on. Marketing is given a 'junior' seat in many board room settings, if it is represented at all.

> "It felt like marketing was put in a back-burner position as the firm put together a small operations committee to discuss response to this shutdown. Unfortunately, they did not include marketing on that committee to help guide internal and external communications and customer engagement. Indeed, I was informed that I should stop with those efforts."
> Anonymous

The perception is: when the hit rate is high, marketing is working; when the hit rate declines, it is not. When backlogs begin to dry up, the knee-jerk reaction is to chase more work, 'Go' questionable leads, jump into new territories. The pace of work accelerates, and the number of proposals goes up, even as the volume of likely 'wins' goes down. Marketing staff find themselves overwhelmed with proposals—morale suffers knowing that low- and no-probability pursuits are eating into their workloads. QA/QC takes a back seat, burn out occurs, technical staff get frustrated. As the losses pile up, the profit margins fall, and the cost spent on marketing staff and resources is scrutinized. This is when layoffs can begin to occur.

> "They didn't think that marketing really contributed to the long-term health of the firm— they didn't think of us as a facet of business development—we were essentially glorified admin staff who did proposals." – Lindsay D. (Marketing Manager, architecture firm, speaking about a former employer)

Senior-level managers and directors are especially susceptible in these circumstances. When the feeding frenzy for new work—any work—takes hold, it's 'all hands on deck' to put together proposals, which in turn pulls managers and directors away from their core responsibilities and back into 'the trenches'. This impacts their ability to be proactive in market research, strategic planning, and business development activities—the very work necessary to position themselves in a competitive field where every firm is now vying for less work. Couple this with marketing budget reductions and the results can be disastrous.

> "There is always going to be a need for someone to manage brand consistency across all offices. Someone has to own it."
> Melissa C. (Marketing and Business Development professional)

At the heart of marketing is the universal truth that 'share of voice' is intrinsically entwined with 'share of market'. If you alter one, you alter the other.

The "Share of Voice" is the amount of marketing capital you spend versus your competitors. The "Share of Market" is the portion of a market controlled by your company. As stated on the website nielsen.com in an article entitled, "Budgeting for the Upturn—Does Share of Voice Matter?":

> "When a brand's share of voice is greater than its share of market, it is likely to grow its market share in the coming year. Therefore, companies that increase their marketing investment when most others are cutting back have an opportunity to substantially improve the standing of their brands."[2]

So to ask the question again in a different way: Given the relationship between marketing investments and share of market, why do professional services firms wholly dependent on B2B business development sacrifice their business development staff?

### Gutcheck.

Because marketing directors, managers, and proposal coordinators haven't demonstrated that they're proactively prepared to pivot into a recession. And if we're honest with ourselves, we really may *not* be prepared.

---

[2] Nikki Clarke, "Budgeting for the Upturn—Does Share of Voice Matter?," The Neilsen Company (August, 6, 2009). https://www.nielsen.com/us/en/insights/news/2009/budgeting-for-the-upturn-does-share-of-voice-matter.html.

**Because recessions are rare.**

**And complacency is a thing.**

We lull ourselves (and others) into thinking that we are a one-trick pony. We have spent so many years in a reactive mode, awash in opportunities, that the thought of reorienting our energy around strategic, proactive activities can feel intimidating. *Where in the world do we start?*

**When it's all this:**

**There's not enough of this:**

"The most important thing is to continue to get our brand out there—to make sure that when the good economic times come back, we're leading that charge, highlighting the brand consistency and the strategic process that we have been following all along."
Angie C. (Marketing Director, construction firm)

We typically have lists of strategic marketing priorities—but did we really have the time to craft an actionable plan to achieve them? When the teaming partner meetings, events, conferences, and proposals were at peak levels, how many of our long-term priorities fell off the 'To-Do' list? How many meetings did we sit through having to say things like 'We haven't finished up that project, but we're working on it' or 'We haven't made much progress on that since our last check-in'?

It's hard owning up to missed deadlines and promises unkept. It's also hard being on the receiving end of it. And whether we knew it or not, every time we made these statements, every time we lagged further behind, we were eroding confidence from others in our firms. *Do they really know what they're doing?*

Coupled with this is the fact that our technical staff often have no idea how truly busy we are. They see the proposals, they see the event planning, they see the website and social media posts, they see the newsletter. What they don't see is the time-consuming work that happens in the background to ensure successful delivery of all of those activities.

If you're only known for a small fraction of what you do, and that work experiences a significant drop-off (less RFPs, less event planning, etc.), it would be natural for firm leadership to assume you're not achieving full utilization of your time. And when difficult conversations arise about how to save on costs, your role may be appraised based on an incomplete picture of the full breadth of your contributions to the firm.

The general psychology of many A/E/C firms is based on two harmful misconceptions: 1) Marketers are 'overhead' staff whose purpose is simply to fulfill requests of technical staff, and 2) Marketers spend all of their time tracking leads, responding to proposals, organizing quals, coordinating events, and posting content online.

To change the psychology of our firms—to build greater understanding and confidence in the value of marketing—we must combat these misconceptions by educating our firms (and ourselves) about the true role of marketing within an A/E/C firm.

"Why marketing management? They were usually paid more, so those layoffs give you more 'bang for your buck'. The technical staff are delivering a product. Proposal coordinators are delivering a product (proposals). For managers and directors where their role might be less defined (development, branding, messaging, external communications) the deliverable is not always concrete. The rationale is: high level, high pay, and no concrete deliverable that they're contributing to daily operations. I do not agree with that line of thinking, but I saw it taking place in many firms during the Great Recession." – Gregory F. (Marketing and Business Development Manager, engineering/environmental firm)

# CHAPTER THREE

# HOW MARKETING CAN CHANGE FIRM PSYCHOLOGY

"I spent the first 10 years of my career feeling and acting like I was the least important person in the room. 'Yes, I will sacrifice my time.' 'Yes you can get this to me late.' Every job I've taken since then, I've gotten better at realizing that enabling other people at your own expense does not lead to a better work product. I've also felt that people are more respectful when you're not groveling (laughs). I wish I would have been stronger in advocating for myself. I wish I would have realized that I was doing a disservice to every other marketer by devaluing my time." – Kelsey P. (Marketing Manager, engineering firm)

Before we can tackle re-establishing our value to our firms, we need take a moment to reaffirm our value in ourselves. In the day-to-day blur of deadlines, it's easy to lose sight of how *dynamic* and *complex* marketing is in an industry like this. Economic expansions are noisy—flush with opportunity and hectic with proposals. Our steady focus on chasing new work can cause us to lose sight of the enormous value we offer across a spectrum of marketing activities—many of which don't truly activate until a downturn. We need to educate our firm leadership about these critically important activities, but a refresher course for ourselves is also in order. It has, after all, been a *long* time since the last recession.

### Cyclical Marketing Activities Tied to Expansions and Downturns
Economic expansions and recessions are somewhat cyclical in nature. While we can't precisely predict when recessions will occur, we *do* know from past statistics that prior to 2020, we have had 12 recessions since WWII—each lasting an average

length of 11 months. Economic expansions last, on average, 3.2 years—sometimes much longer as we've recently experienced![3] Given that recessions are relatively short in duration, we should table our concern about how long this current recession will last and instead focus on the marketing activities that often languish during expansions.

"What the Great Recession taught us is that we are businesses before we are service firms."
Frank L. (Marketing and Strategy consultant)

These charts demonstrate the fluctuations in marketing activities that can occur depending on what cycle of the economy we find ourselves in. In an expansion, you grow. In a downturn, you stabilize. Depending on which cycle you are in, you must adjust how you approach your work.

| | Economic Expansion | Economic Contraction |
|---|---|---|
| Private Work | ↑ | ↓ |
| Public Work | ↑ | ↓ |
| Proposals | ↑ | ↓ |
| New Office Buildouts | ↑ | ↓ |
| Website Redesign | ↑ | ↓ |
| Conference Attendance | ↑ | ↑ |
| Teaming Partner / Client Outreach | ↑ | ↑ |
| Teaming Partner / Client Audits | ↓ | ↑ |
| Office Consolidation | ↓ | ↑ |
| Website Refinements | ↓ | ↑ |
| Staff Training | ↓ | ↑ |
| Industry Research | ↓ | ↑ |

[3] "US Business Cycle Expansions and Contractions," *National Bureau of Economic Research.* https://www.nber.org/cycles.html.

**System Stabilization**

Internal Style Guide Refinement

Process Documentation

Time Allocation Reviews

Competitor Audits

Social Media Audits

New Marketplace Development

Staff: Personal Brand Mentoring

Billable Work: Editing, report layout, writing

Industry Research

For instance, as a firm grows, expands its services, or gains a deeper market share, major updates or a complete overhaul of the website may be necessary. This costs time and money, including content generation, front- and back-end web development, user experience (UX) evaluation, a branding refresh, and navigation of assets from the old site to the new one. Because it's a significant financial investment, most website overhauls occur during expansions when year-end profits are healthy and leadership have the appetite to take on the cost. Conversely, a recession provides a valuable opportunity to take a breath and assess the new website with fresh eyes. This is the time to work out bugs and make refinements such as special messaging about your firm's response to the recession, more detailed information about your workplace culture, or enhanced project descriptions that orient your work for a recession-focused audience.

Another example concerns teaming partner relationships. In expansions we strengthen existing relationships, but also establish new ones. We expand our network of potential partners and take chances on new firms. On the flip side, in recessions many firms become cautious—forming alliances with familiar partners, often with less appetite for partnering with unproven firms. There is less work to pursue and more firms pursuing it. This hyper-competitive environment warrants a close examination of all partners (as well as your competition!)—who's winning, who's too expensive, who's overstayed their welcome with a particular client. Our firm leaders are hungry for information like this.

> "Firms are looking to Marketing to help answer the questions
> that they don't know the answers to."
> Bonnie T. (Strategic Pursuit Manager, environmental/water engineering firm)

Prioritizing your recession marketing time to such activities demonstrates to your leadership a heightened sense of awareness of marketing cycles and shifts your focus to the 'stabilizing' tasks to take on when markets contract.

## Marketing Functions

You can have a room full of musicians orchestrating their instruments or you can have a room full of musicians playing at random. One produces a symphony. The other produces noise. In many marketing departments we spend a disproportionate amount of time responding to RFPs and significantly less effort on other critical forms of marketing. During expansions, we are so focused on chasing the work that it's easy to 'zoom in' on this one facet of the overall marketing construct—devoting all of our mental energy to it while other marketing functions languish. We start to think of ourselves solely as 'proposal' coordinators instead of 'marketing' coordinators.

**We see and think this:**

## When it's actually this:

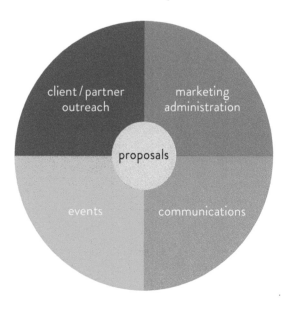

## Surrounded by this:

competitor evals

teaming negotiations

client outreach

lunch and learns

coffee check-ins

conference networking

event attendance
+ sponsorship

event development

event sponsorships

speaking engagements

philanthropic giving

job fairs

boilerplate updates

data entry

client surveys

leads tracking

editorial + layout

data visualization

media interviews

white papers

op-eds

newsletter

advertising

social media

website

client / partner
outreach

marketing
administration

proposals

events

communications

We forget that while proposals are at the heart of an A/E/C marketing department's 'engine' this core service is surrounded and supported by four key foundational functions: marketing administration, client and partner outreach, communications, and events.

Each of these foundational functions is comprised of a key set of tasks and activities. These are efforts that your marketing team is no doubt deeply familiar with, but when viewed as a whole, it is easier to see how one function supports another (e.g. A well-organized and maintained asset database makes it easy to pull content for client meetings and online postings. An opinion piece or blog post helps position a staffer as a panelist at an upcoming event. Steady attendance at industry events provides opportunities to meet with prospective partners and arrange for future one-on-one meetings to discuss potential teaming arrangements.)

As often happens in firms that view marketing as simply 'fulfillment' staff, these functions are seen more as 'one-offs' and not part of a complex nervous system that benefits from regular oversight and maintenance. And even in firms where marketing staff are directly tasked with outreach, communications, events coordination, or data entry, these 'hats' tend to slip off easily when the RFPs come flooding in.

"Evidence from past recessions supports the wisdom of keeping marketing departments intact. Companies making a knee-jerk reaction by cutting their marketing staff in a recession will likely be among the last to recover once the economy improves"
Michael R. (Public Relations and Marketing, independent consultant)

Help your firm's leadership visualize the marketing engine as a whole. They must see how these activities relate to each other and understand that while it *might* be possible to tackle them at random, what they'll ultimately end up with is a room full of noise and not the symphony they crave. Help them understand that these functions work in service of the creation of well-conceived, high-probability proposals, as well as a brand that is amplified to its fullest in your marketplaces.

Once your firm's decision-makers begin to appreciate how powerful a marketing department can be when all the functions are orchestrated, their perception of marketing will begin to shift. This is particularly helpful during a recession—for when the number of proposals fall, the team will know how (and where) to shift their collective energy.

A final consideration: knowing that these functions exist and are interrelated is not enough. To put this into action, you'll need to assign 'champions' for each area. *See Chapter 6: Staff Assessment and Cross-Training* for more information.

"Marketing influences absolutely everything in the world. Marketing is not only at the table in other industries, they are the number 3 or 4 person in the organization."
Damion M. (Proposal Manager, construction firm)

# CHAPTER 4

# WE'RE IN A RECESSION, NOW WHAT?

*"The thing that scares me is wondering how long the contraction is going to last.
We're going to have a whole year before we know what fiscal budgets will look like."*
Kelsey P. (Marketing Manager, engineering firm)

Unlike past recessions, the recession of 2020 will be remembered for the shock at how quickly it impacted the A/E/C industry across all sectors. Firms finished up 2019 with record-breaking profits—many with thoughts of expansion into new markets, headhunting talent to open up new service areas, building out new office space, investing in new technologies, or all of the above. Marketing professionals were advancing in their careers with successful negotiations for wage increases and promotions. Job boards were filled with announcements for proposal coordinators and strategic thinkers as firms sought to shore up the demand and opportunities that kept rolling in the door.

Many firms had just completed strategic plans with confidence, built on the spoils of an economic expansion that lasted over 10 years—the longest in U.S. history. And while signs were already indicating that a recession was imminent due to a slowdown in global manufacturing and volatility in oil prices, few firms in the A/E/C industry gave this much attention as they continued to see new work hit their pipelines. Ambitious, multi-year projects were being dreamed up at the state and local levels, many fueled by multimillion-dollar bond measures (recently passed in large metro regions throughout the country)—all of which would provide ample opportunity for project work in transportation, affordable housing, K-12, and so on. The private sector was booming, with cranes in hot demand and construction costs at an all-time high. And all of this with an unemployment rate of 3.8%—one of the lowest rates of unemployment since WWII.

The pressure on marketing departments was enormous. Firm confidence fueled an appetite for growth—both in terms of market share and in brand recognition. Websites were blown up and recreated and firms vied for top sponsorship placements. A focus on 'internal marketing' developed as firms competed for talent in a shrinking job pool. Ideas to enhance corporate culture and outward appearance were channeled to marketing at every angle, from new swag to newsletters to demand for more frequent new content on social media. Requests for cut sheets, brochures, and other stylized quals also added to the workload.

> And all the while, leads and RFPs kept flooding in,
> in wave after wave.

Most marketing professionals I spoke with for this book said that for the past several years it was all they could do to just to keep their heads above water.

Now here we find ourselves—watching the tide go out and we're left standing on the shoreline. Where once we were almost drowning, we now are stranded on the sand.

"With COVID-19, my job kind of switched from constantly doing proposals to all of a sudden having time to focus on the strategic initiatives that had been moved to the back burner."
Angie C. (Marketing Director, construction firm)

We've spent years in reactive mode simply trying to figure out how to get things done. Now we find ourselves trying to prioritize a large backlog of marketing tasks while also dreaming up creative ways to bring in new work. As the recession deepens and our profit margins shrink, our firms will be forced to make tough financial decisions. In the meantime, we're left wondering: How can marketing play a role in protecting our company and protecting our jobs? How can we best position ourselves for when the tide comes back in?

The rest of this book provides strategies and key action steps your team can take—both in direct reaction to the recession and as part of an annual list of activities that will strengthen your team's bonds as well as Marketing's value within the firm.

> "The main difference between this recession and the last recession is that people kept to themselves last time. They kept their cards close to their chest. Now it feels like a community. You feel like you're going through this together."
> Kelly J. (Marketing Director, civil engineering and planning firm)

# FOUR RECESSION ACTION STEPS

"Since the shutdown, my job has changed. Event season didn't happen—March, April, May, and June were always our heaviest parts of the year—attending conventions and events and engaging with clients that way. It all just sort of stopped. I had a sobering moment where I had to ask myself, 'What do I do now?' (laughs) But I was able to pull out the strategic plan we had just created at the end of 2019 and dug in, working on things I never had time for when times were busy." – Jewel B. (Business Development Manager, engineering firm)

Unlike past recessions, which were driven in large part by over-leveraged financial markets and a coinciding drop in consumer confidence, this one hit us like a ton of bricks. In a year that began with record-breaking profits and seemingly endless opportunities, a global pandemic forced governments to abruptly shut down life as we knew it. Schools closed, retail stores and restaurants shuttered, and corporate organizations were compelled to shut down their offices—with each individual worker left to rig up office space in their new work-from-home status.

From the comfort of our living rooms we watched as in-person events were canceled and worked our way through rescinding sponsorships and trying to get earmarked marketing dollars back in the door. We met over video conference and tried to establish a new 'normal' in how to triage work and craft responses and messaging on our firm's behalf. We listened intently to our firm leadership in virtual 'all-staffs' eager to know what steps they would take in shoring up resources in the face of a coming recession.

"There are two types of professionals in a firm—people who bill and generate revenue and those of us who support the revenue-producer steams. In the recent expansion, billable professionals were stretched to the limit by their deadlines and client needs. This provided an opportunity for Marketing to shine—it showed how marketing staff could expand their roles and help with client relations, coaching, and professional development."
Michael R. (Public Relations and Marketing, independent consultant)

As marketers, we are by nature communicators and 'fixers'. We feel a growing sense of urgency and want to help support our firms. We want to be the bearers of useful information—both to be part of the solution, but to also demonstrate our value.

However, when the path forward is murky—with uncertainties and twists in the road that we can't yet see—a form of mental paralysis can take hold. *Where do we begin?*

What follows are four immediate action steps you can take to get your bearings, reinforce your team's confidence, and demonstrate to your leadership that you are *proactively* positioning your marketing resources as the first line of defense (and offense) as the markets begin to contract.

These 'recession responses' are meant to be done in order, with key takeaways shared and discussed at your marketing check-ins and useful insights shared with your firm leadership.

## Recession Responses

1. Check-up Checklist Assessment

2. Marketing Staff Assessment and Cross-Training

3. Historical Analysis of the Great Recession

4. Marketing Report-Backs

"You want to keep as many marketers around as you can when the bubble bursts because they're the chasers." – Cheryl N. (Business Development Manager, architecture firm)

# CHAPTER FIVE

# RECESSION RESPONSE #1
# THE 'CHECK-UP' CHECKLIST ASSESSMENT

"When I started, we were more in reactionary mode with the intent of wanting to be more strategic. But we lacked the organization to do that. The firm had great ideas, but not enough follow-through or accountability. I took on that role to try to coalesce these ideas and create plans of action and follow-through." – Craig R. (Marketing Manager, architecture firm)

We have been so busy for so long responding to RFPs that many other facets of marketing have taken a back seat. It's difficult to even know where to begin. The first step in tackling the big question 'Where do we prioritize our time?' is understanding what parts of your marketing engine have languished or been underdeveloped while your proposal pipeline was maxed out.

To begin to wrap your head around this, you must do a needs assessment. Filling out a Marketing Check-up Checklist allows you to take a step back and critically analyze where your systems are developed and where they aren't. This checklist provides a range of marketing assets, services, and activities that are common in most marketing departments—whether you're a team of one or many. Schedule a time to print out a checklist like this. Quietly sit down and assess each item—dispassionate and without defense. If you are part of a larger team, do it together in a group exercise and compare your answers. This isn't the time to discuss why these items have been left unaddressed—it's the time to wrap your heads around all the good work to be done now that you finally have time to do it.

Once you have a list of items in need of development or refinement, begin to prioritize and assign tasks. Do some tasks take special knowledge or design skills? Do some require research or buy-in from the leadership? Determine what the basic needs are for each item, then assign them based on each team member's unique strengths, interests, and skillsets.[4]

Don't yet have a good understanding of what those are? The next step—the Marketing Staff Assessment—will help you sort and discover where each of your team members are (or should be) spending their time. Conducting a staff assessment will help reveal where your team's strengths are and where they need to be defined and developed.

> "Form a path that runs alongside what you're doing that creates additional value. If you're doing lots of proposals and SOQs, learn CRM or learn to develop marketing plans, or get experience in business development. Diversify your skill set in visible ways to your firm leadership." – Gregory F. (Marketing and Business Development Manager, engineering/environmental firm)

---

[4] To download a free copy of this checklist, please visit: www.gonogoconsulting.com

# The 'Check-Up' Checklist Assessment

| DOES YOUR MARKETING DEPARTMENT: | YES | INCONSISTENT/ INCOMPLETE | NO |
|---|---|---|---|
| Have an annual off-site marketing retreat? | | | |
| Have a specified marketing budget for events, sponsorships, memberships, etc? | | | |
| Have dedicated time codes for marketing broken down by specific tasks? | | | |
| Annually review where marketing staff are billing time? | | | |
| Provide office/firmwide trainings on house style, proposal process, how to network, other in-demand skill-building exercises? | | | |
| Have a marketing internship program? | | | |
| Have contacts at relevant local media outlets in each of your marketplaces? | | | |
| Have a press release template? | | | |
| Have a process for conducting competitor research? | | | |
| Have complete dossier on each of your main competitors? | | | |
| Track how many proposals you do by month, by prime/sub? | | | |
| Have a style guide? | | | |
| Secure speaking engagements for your key staff? | | | |
| Have a documented process for coordinating a free or low-cost event? | | | |
| Have a documented process for coordinating a high-budget event? | | | |
| Host tables/sponsor events in your key market areas? | | | |
| Prepare quarterly reports for your firm leadership? | | | |
| Does your Marketing Director have regularly scheduled briefings with your CEO? | | | |

| DOES EVERYONE ON YOUR TEAM: | YES | INCONSISTENT/ INCOMPLETE | NO |
|---|---|---|---|
| Know how to update the website? | | | |
| Know how to copyedit (using the same style)? | | | |
| Have full command of your CRM software? | | | |
| Know how to use InDesign? | | | |
| Know how to use PPT? | | | |
| Can every person on your team recite your firm's strategic plan by heart? | | | |
| Does everyone on your team have an 'alter ego'? Are they tasked with and committed to overseeing a marketing function(s) beyond proposal work? | | | |

CLEAR OUT THE COBWEBS:
What are the "We'll get around to it" items that reflect poorly on your department?

| | | |
|---|---|---|
| Unfiled boilerplate piling up | | Dormant social media accounts |
| Glitchy templates that billable staff hate | | Outdated news section on website |
| Outdated color palettes | | Typos in staff resumes that never get fixed |
| Inconsistent branding (Word, PPT, InDesign, website, etc.) | | Messy or inconsistent filing system for marketing materials |

# CHAPTER SIX

# RECESSION RESPONSE #2
## STAFF ASSESSMENT
## AND CROSS TRAINING

"The agile marketer adapts and configures their role around the unique characteristics of the firm they are at." – Michael R. (Public Relations and Marketing, independent consultant)

Marketing coordinators are often seen as 'the people who put our proposals together'. The Business Development staff are often seen as 'the people who attend events and take other people out for coffee'. It's understandable—our technical staff only see what we allow them to. They are not typically in our marketing check-in meetings. They aren't privy to the conversations and actions that build up to the marketing activities they participate in. They see the quals, but maybe not the database and maintenance behind it. They see the logo up at the breakfast event, but maybe not the email coordination, design, and content writing that goes into the sponsorship. They see that we have a LinkedIn account, but not the push and pull of finding and creating content to promote our brand.

Like a duck gliding across the pond, they can't see the rigorous paddling happening under the surface.

And ironically, sometimes neither can we. In the course of each busy day, it's difficult to remember that every action we take, email we send, template we create, or competitor we evaluate is a task that cleanly falls into a basic category—a function—of marketing.

These functions are distinct, but interrelated. They cannot exist in a vacuum separate from each other, but each takes focused dedication to develop and maintain.

In each function there are a variety of discrete tasks that have to be tended to. For many of us, these happen organically and oftentimes haphazardly. Like a leaky plumbing system, we spend our time being reactionary, dealing with leaks one at a time as they become a problem. The water still comes out of the tap, but if there are breakdowns in the system, you don't know you have a problem until you have a moldy mess on your hands.

"People in marketing that are 100% anything are seen as replaceable with a few exceptions. You have to be able to deliver the concrete deliverables but also offer intrinsic value that is hard to replace when you take it all as a whole. Add value with horizontal integration—don't get stuck in just the vertical work of proposals, tracking, interview prep, and debriefs. Get outside that cycle of procurement. Find the gaps at your firm where there is help needed in other types of marketing activities." – Gregory F. (Marketing and Business Development Manager engineering/environmental firm)

To prevent this from happening, it is critical that each member of your team have a well-rounded understanding of each marketing function and how they interact. Each staffer should have enough knowledge and training to shift their focus from proposal work to activities within each function. Cross training staff across this spectrum builds in agility and allows marketing resources to pivot in a proactive way. This ensures that if overall proposal workload decreases, staff have the ability to quickly turn to other tasks which benefit the firm and can be reported back to the leadership.

It is also critical that each function have a dedicated champion. For those who are the sole marketers for their firms, this means being a champion of time. For those that have multiple marketing staff, this means assigning roles of oversight, with your manager or director checking in regularly to make sure each function is operating smoothly.

Just as with the Check-Up Checklist, you must assess your marketing functions and determine who is overseeing them. There can be overlap in who performs the discrete tasks within each function (for instance, it is often everyone's responsibility to make sure new project descriptions make it back into the quals database), but there should be a marketing staffer responsible for tending to the overall health and operations of each function.

Not only will this provide critical insight into where and how to devote staff resources, it will help ensure that the marketing activities that technical staff and leadership *do* see are performed and executed smoothly and efficiently. At all times, but especially during downturns, inefficiency raises attention and scrutiny from firm decision makers. Inefficiency draws negative attention to the marketing department, making it much easier for non-marketing professionals to feel compelled to step in and 'fix' things.

> "Find a project that lights you up and makes the firm better. If you love organizing things, do it. If it's talking to your coworkers and getting white papers out, do it. Find your passion project and show your firm how you add value beyond proposals."
>
> Lindsay D. (Marketing Manager, architecture firm)

## Roles of the Champions

### ▪ Marketing Administration

Do you thrive on organization? Do well-conceived and sorted file structures make you happy? Do you enjoy being the person who knows where everything 'lives'? Can you see the interconnected web of systems that tie together all of your marketing assets? Then the Marketing Administration champion role is for you.

In this role you catalogue and assess the filing systems, marketing guides, templates, resumes, quals, photos, graphics, and leads tracking processes for marketing. You create naming conventions and consistency in how items are organized. You look for ways to reduce the amount of time it takes to find things and ensure that newly created content makes its way back into the database. This may be a series of files living on a server, a fully integrated CRM system, an intranet, online spreadsheets, or a combination of all of them. Whatever your system is, you know it down to its DNA, and you constantly look for ways to improve upon it.

### ▪ Communications

Do you like to write? To tell the story of what makes your firm and your project work special? Do you find yourself thinking of ways to broadcast your firm's knowledge to your clients and teaming partners? Do you understand the power of social media and the importance of telling the story of the meaningful work your firm does? Then you are the Communications champion.

In this role you look for opportunities to elevate the firm's brand. You identify and seek out the 'storytellers' in your firm. You assess the technical staff and look for what makes each of them special. You assess your firm's brand and tease out what sets it apart from the competition. You learn the firm's value statements and infuse them into the boilerplate you use on proposals and incorporate them into messages you broadcast on your website and social media feeds. You sit down with senior leadership to learn about the history of the firm, major contributions your company has made to the state of the practice. You inspire, cajole, and pester technical staff to take time to share their own thoughts online and in white papers. In essence, you help make sure that the *meaning and value* of the work your firm does doesn't get lost in the day-to-day billing of projects.

### Events

Do you love getting people in a room together? Do you find satisfaction in the hum of a crowd all talking to each other and finding common ground? Do you look for ways to coalesce your network of teaming partners and clients into situations that build trust and inspire relationships? Do you love to throw a good party? Then the Event champion role is for you.

You understand that magic can happen when people get out of the office and into congregation. They eat and drink, laugh, and take a breath from the billable work. Technical staff are reminded that their identity goes beyond the next project. As the Events Champion, you are constantly on the lookout for events that spark inspiration and that celebrate your field. You look for ways to get your technical staff up on the stage, on the panel, in front of the podium. You purchase tables for events then think through the perfect mix of your best rainmakers, emerging young professionals, and clients and teaming partners. You go a step further and think of ways you can partner with others to bring people together, holding cocktail mixers and hosting webinars. You seek out trusted nonprofits and industry organizations that celebrate and positively impact your field and you align your brand with theirs, sponsoring their events and showing up in support. You understand that your visibility out in the community makes (and keeps) you relevant—that every time a potential teaming partner or client sees your logo they are seeing you as an engaged and enthusiastic industry partner.

## ■ Client and Partner Outreach

Have you been in the industry long enough to know who all the key players are? Do you thrive on making connections, grabbing coffee with colleagues, and enriching your relationships with them? Can you prattle off the names of clients and teaming partners with ease in Go/No-Go conversations? Can you point to articles that detail upcoming project opportunities in your marketplaces? Do you follow the funding cycles of local governments and monitor the news for what projects are coming down the pipeline? Do you know all the gossip about who left what firm and who just launched a new startup? Who jumped from consulting to a public agency and vice versa? When you're at events do you readily spot several people you know, exchanging smiles and hellos and the latest about your family trip, your new house, the puppy you just adopted? In short, has your job and your life become entwined to the point that the personal and the professional have overlapped? Then the Client and Partner Outreach champion role is for you.

In this role you document your universe of contacts. You know which technical staff have which relationships and where. You help with relationship succession when senior staff retire and you engage deeply with marketing staff at other firms. You regularly call key contacts to see how they're doing. You watch the leads come in the door and immediately start thinking about firms to team with. You make note of new firms or key partners where the relationship is underdeveloped, and you look for ways to engage and build trust. To you, every cold call has to potential of leading to a new friendship and you long ago surpassed 500 connections on LinkedIn. You're active in SMPS and industry-specific organizations and you keep a busy schedule that has you out of the office as much as you're in it. More than anything, you love your company, your culture and values, the breadth of the work you do, and you *constantly* look for ways to get others as excited about your company as you are.

Once you sort out who your champions are, the real work begins—to strengthen the ties between each function and look for the interrelated ways that each function supports the efforts of the others.

# CHAPTER SEVEN

# RECESSION RESPONSE #3
## HISTORICAL ANALYSIS OF THE GREAT RECESSION

Now that you find yourself facing down an uncertain pipeline, it's time to ask the tough questions: where will the work dry up and where will it stay steady? With the high rate of turnover and leapfrogging that happens in the marketing world, most coordinators, managers, and even directors were not working at their firms during the last recession. Even those that were find their recollection of that time hazy and disjointed.

> "If I could go back to the firm I was working at in 2012, I would have elbowed my way into management meetings and given voice to ways to navigate our way out of the recession, not just report on the number of proposals we were going after."
> Frank L. (Marketing and Strategy Consultant)

To grapple with the tough questions of what comes next, it is critical to look back and analyze how the firm pulled through last time. While it is true that many types of work dry up during a recession, there is always work to be done—often smaller in scale and perhaps not as exciting and grand as when times are flush. But in the lean times, it's the 'bread and butter' type of work that saw a lot of firms through the depths of the recession. And now that there's a heightened state of anxiety forming at the top levels, one of the most valuable and demonstrative contributions the marketing team can undertake is an analysis of market and service-area performance that occurred the last time a recession took place.

The nuts and bolts of doing this are not typically difficult. All firms, big and small must account for past project work. This is often found on an internal intranet or CRM system. Doing a search query for a particular timeframe is usually just a matter of mouse clicks. And the information to be found can provide a treasure trove of data that can inform future business development strategies.

"If I could go back pre-recession and change anything I would advocate for more data and have it available at my fingertips. I would have pushed for CRM implementation back when there weren't financial constraints so that I have that information now. For the leadership, the perception here is: marketing is not related to operations. I know I need to have these conversations, but it would easier to have real data to back up that argument, not just my feelings." – Connie G. (Business Development Manager, commercial contracting firm)

### How to Pull Historic Data and What to Look For
Start by pulling data from just before the last recession to the following two years after. In the case of the Great Recession, this would be from about 2007 through to 2011. Initially you want a list of all proposals and projects. If possible, pull the name of the project, the service area, the project lead (you may find that the principal or manager of the project is no longer with the company, but for those that are still on the payroll, this can be helpful in understanding their trajectory of work). Pull data that notes if the project was a priming or subbing effort, the geography, the dollar amount, and if the work was competitive or sole-sourced.

Once you have this, you will no doubt find yourself with a very large amount of information! If you work at an especially large firm with several disciplines, this exercise should be done separately for each type of work you perform.

When you have the data in spreadsheet form, you are ready to start your analysis. Key findings should include:

▶ # of proposals by year

▶ Hit rate

▶ Fluctuations in priming versus subbing

▶ Public versus private work

▶ Dollar averages (and note the outliers)

▶ RFP versus sole source

▶ Type of public work: local, state, federal

▶ Type of private work

▶ Ratio of public to private work

Do you notice a drop-off or increase is certain types of services? Any patterns that emerge that point to types of work that seem sensitive to recession or are 'recession-proof'?

Generate a list of statistics and key takeaways that you can build into a report for your firm leadership. If the data is telling you that certain kinds of work experienced a significant drop-off while other areas remained consistent, this should inform your client engagement and outreach strategy. Perhaps this means that you take a look at what services you're accentuating on your website or perhaps it triggers phone calls to key clients that procure this type of work. This type of analysis will give you as much of a crystal ball into what opportunities may arise as anything you read in the industry publications.

> "Our strategy should not be to simply go after more proposals."
> Kelsey P. (Marketing Manager, engineering firm)

The other benefit of this type of analysis is that it puts a fine point on your overall hit rate. During recessions, marketers often comment that a wave of desperation seems to infuse Go/No-Go conversations. In an attempt to fill the backlog, technical staff relax their standards and opt to chase work that they are neither well-positioned for, known for, or truly experienced in. This anxiety-induced pursuit of work generally takes a big toll on overall hit rate and creates unfortunate opportunity cost for more viable project pursuits. Being able to point to declines in hit rates can help marketers make a viable case for maintaining Go/No-Go standards, which in turn decreases the number of 'lame duck' proposals that gobble up resources.

"When you have no options, you go for every option. When times are tough you throw the Go/No-Go theory out the door and you chase anything that moves."
Cheryl N. (Business Development Manager, architecture firm)

Once the analysis is complete, present it to your leadership team in concert with a general report on your team's emerging recession-oriented strategy (informed by the Check-up Checklist and Staff Assessment). Read on for more on the topic of reporting in the fourth and final Recession Action step.

# CHAPTER EIGHT

# RECESSION RESPONSE #4
## MARKETING REPORT-BACKS

"I am convinced that the way marketing directors and marketing managers preserve their
roles is to be true bearers of valuable information. They have to come into leadership
meetings with data and market insights that are meaningful and can help direct the firm."
Frank L. (Marketing and Strategy consultant)

For the marketing directors reading this book (and others who have a built-in expectation that they will report on marketing activities to firm leadership), ask yourself: how frequent and meaningful has your reporting been? We all start with the best of intentions when we begin a new job. In the beginning, we typically have ample time to build out our role—this is the planning phase and where we set the ground rules. We set expectations with our bosses across a range of metrics, including regular reports on marketing activities and progress made toward our business development strategies.

But the truth is: we get busy. Days, weeks, and months can slip by, with the bulk of our time going to an ever-present array of fire drills. Soon you find yourself with a backlog of reporting—which takes time you feel like you don't have. And all the while this radio silence is noticed by the leadership. They too are busy with their own jobs, but the absence of good reporting from Marketing doesn't go unnoticed and they may not be proactive in asking for it. But they're aware of the absence. Indeed, they may be watching the calendar and noting the irregularities in reporting. They may be forming judgments about your abilities to act as a sentinel and they may start leaving you out of critical conversations about firm strategy.

"Make sure that you stand out. Don't blend in. Generally speaking, it's easy for marketers in A/E/C to stay in our lane, to not speak up to the leadership."
Damion M. (Proposal Manager, construction firm)

This can lead to a general lack of confidence that can directly impact the role you will play when it comes time to make difficult decisions about cost-saving measures.

It is critical that your firm's leadership be kept informed of the hard work and dedication of your marketing team. They need to know what's keeping you busy; the non-proposal-related activities that you're devoting time to. They need to see the value you are infusing into the work. They need to know that you have a plan and that you're implementing it.

"One of the messages we've been trying to give to our management team and our seller/doers is that it's time to get hungry again. We need to be in front of our clients—creating and building relationships, be top of mind." – McKenzie R. (Marketing Manager, engineering firm)

If upon reading this you can honestly say you haven't been pro-active in transmitting updates to your firm leadership, now is the time to shake the rust off your reporting.

The first step in doing this is acknowledging the need for more frequent reporting. Before you go off and earmark large sections of your time, you need to get clear with your bosses about what they want and need. Set a meeting with your direct supervisor and state your intention to gather up data, have a list of metrics you intend to report on and get buy-off on the list. The last thing you want to do is spin your wheels on research and analysis that the leadership isn't going to appreciate. Make sure they know what you're doing and when they can expect to see a full report. Effective reporting takes time—and given that time is at a premium (indeed valued down to the minute), your firm leaders need to agree that this is a 'valuable' use of your time.

"It was a very small group that set company direction. Strategic plans were not shared with
Marketing or even the management group as a whole. I would ask 'what are our business
goals, what are our growth targets'—I was hungry for data. We could have developed stronger,
more comprehensive plans to support those corporate initiatives if we had access."
Melissa C. (Marketing/Business Development professional, speaking about a former employer)

Come ready with a list of metrics you want to track. Consider it a 'marketing flyover' that views each metric through the lens of business development. Ask yourself: Is this helping us build our brand and capture new work? Are our resources being used to their fullest potential?

This list of metrics could include:

▶ Proposals (number opened, priming vs. subbing, $ amounts, and active win-loss rate from the previous quarter)

▶ Website traffic

▶ Earned media

▶ Glassdoor reviews

▶ Upcoming presentations by staff

▶ Whitepapers or blog posts that are in the works

▶ Sponsored events

▶ Upcoming conferences

▶ Special projects (this can include updates on major initiatives the firm has undertaken: new office openings, a website overhaul, rebranding, etc.)

The format of the reporting can be a simple oral summary at a check-in, a written document, or bullets on PPT slides. Determine the format and level of detail that your firm leaders will most appreciate. Be careful not to go overboard, hitting them with too much detail. You need to strike a balance between transmitting valuable information that aids decision-making and flooding them with so much detail that they tune out.

# TEN ESSENTIAL ANNUAL TASKS

"We're shaking the bushes, digging up the trees, pulling up the lawn, looking everywhere for new work." – Damion M. (Proposal Manager, construction firm)

Just like the instructions you get on an airplane to put your own oxygen mask on before helping others, the four action steps outlined in the previous chapters require immediate attention when a firm enters a recession. Once you've tackled those, it's time to review the activities and exercises you should conduct and revisit on an annual basis, regardless of what's going on in the market. These steps serve to bring your team together, create shared understanding of goals and priorities, help you triage your time, and make the best use of your finite resources.

While many of these steps can be done in tandem, you should generally conduct them in order, assigning tasks to staff that have best availability, interest, and skillset. Key takeaways from each step should be shared and discussed at your marketing check-ins and useful insights shared with your firm leadership.

Some of these are fairly quick and easy, some take time and collaboration with your team. Estimated hours are provided for each activity.

## Ten Essential Annual Tasks

1. Know Your Flow: Calculating Proposal Peaks

2. Creating the Essential Calendar

3. It Takes a Village: Dialing in Staff Roles and Responsibilities

4. The Critical Value of Interns

5. Tighten Up Leads Tracking

6. The Client Survey

7. Digital Marketing: Reach Your Audience Without Wasting Your Time

8. Establish (or Refine) Your Marketing Budget

9. Creating Transparency in Your Marketing Tasks

10. Retreat!

# CHAPTER NINE

# KNOW YOUR FLOW:
# CALCULATING PROPOSAL PEAKS

*"Honestly, it feels like there are so many proposals happening, but we have a lot of projects that we know still have to get done. We've had to pull in technical, billable staff to help on marketing tasks they wouldn't normally work on just to help us with some of these projects to keep them moving forward while we're responding to proposals."*
Lindsay D. (Marketing Manager, architecture firm)

Every year brings new initiatives, opportunities, and change. Senior professionals retire, websites get blown up, marketing staff have major life events that pull them out of the office. There are holiday parties and newsletters to plan, new social media initiatives to implement, and branding exercises that see us revamping our old templates or rethinking our logos. There is an exhaustive list of marketing-related activities that require careful thought and planning—all of which have to be done in concert with the ongoing influx of proposal work.

Often, we try to work in strategic marketing exercises 'when we have time'. But that light week you had a few months back, where you cleared your calendar to think through implementation or to start tackling a project, all too often leads to stalled projects and lost momentum when yet again you have a pile of RFPs hit the pipeline.

How do you combat this? How do you ensure that important marketing initiatives don't perpetually take a backseat to the reactive rhythm of proposal response?

The first step is understanding that 'when you have time' will never be something you can rely on until you understand the unique rhythm of your firm. Whether your firm is 100% driven by public work, a mix of public and private, mostly priming efforts or a subconsultant to others, there is a tidal nature to the opportunities you chase—driven by the funding cycles of your clients. While it can be tricky to determine the individual fiscal calendars of each and every client, doing an analysis of the number of active proposals by month can help you start to wrap your head around when your peak proposal times occur.

And once you know when those are, you can move on to *Chapter 10: Creating Your Annual Marketing Calendar.*

### ⏱ Timekeeper: 2-4 hours

Whether you're using CRM software or some other internal accounting system, you shouldn't have too much trouble pulling a list of all proposals that were opened in the last three years. The process goes like this:

**Step 1:** Conduct a search query of all proposals opened (regardless of win-loss rate) for the last three years, making sure to capture the date that the proposal code was created. Download this information into an Excel spreadsheet.

| Proposal | Date Opened |
|---|---|
| Port East Alignment Analysis | 1/3/19 |
| Professional Services On-Call | 1/1/19 |
| ROW Analysis | 1/9/19 |
| Downtown Area Plan | 1/10/19 |
| Community Plan | 1/25/19 |
| Commercial Corridors Strategy | 1/16/19 |
| Madison Station | 1/15/19 |
| South Downtown Zoning Analysis | 1/18/18 |
| Economic Prosperity | 1/1/19 |
| I-96 Feasibility Study | 1/1/19 |

**Step 2:** Remove any extraneous information per entry, keeping only the month the proposal was created. Open three new tabs in your Excel file and label them 'Year 1', 'Year 2', and 'Year 3'.

| Date Opened | | | | | |
|---|---|---|---|---|---|
| 1/3/19 | | | | | |
| 1/1/19 | | | | | |
| 1/9/19 | | | | | |
| 1/10/19 | | | | | |
| 1/25/19 | | | | | |
| 1/16/19 | | | | | |
| 1/15/19 | | | | | |
| 1/18/18 | | | | | |
| 1/1/19 | | | | | |
| 1/1/19 | | | | | |
| Year 1 | Year 2 | Year 3 | | | |

**Step 3:** In the Year 1 tab, write the name of each month (January, February, March, and so on) down an adjacent column. Copy this over to Year 2 and Year 3.

| Date Opened | Monthly Tally | | | | |
|---|---|---|---|---|---|
| 1/3/19 | January | | | | |
| 1/1/19 | February | | | | |
| 1/9/19 | March | | | | |
| 1/10/19 | April | | | | |
| 1/25/19 | May | | | | |
| 1/16/19 | June | | | | |
| 1/15/19 | July | | | | |
| 1/18/18 | August | | | | |
| 1/1/19 | September | | | | |
| 1/1/19 | October | | | | |
| Year 1 | Year 2 | Year 3 | | | |

**Step 4:** For Year 1, manually count and enter in the number of proposals (both priming and subbing) that were opened in each month of that year and put the tallies in the cell next to each month. Repeat this for Year 2 and Year 3.

| Date Opened | Monthly Tally | | | | |
|---|---|---|---|---|---|
| 1/3/19 | January | 26 | | | |
| 1/1/19 | February | 37 | | | |
| 1/9/19 | March | 37 | | | |
| 1/10/19 | April | 32 | | | |
| 1/25/19 | May | 21 | | | |
| 1/16/19 | June | 36 | | | |
| 1/15/19 | July | 19 | | | |
| 1/18/18 | August | 21 | | | |
| 1/1/19 | September | 26 | | | |
| 1/1/19 | October | 35 | | | |
| Year 1 | Year 2 | Year 3 | | | |

**Step 5:** Once you have inputted all of the tallies, select the cells, click 'Insert', then 'chart' option, and select the column graph.

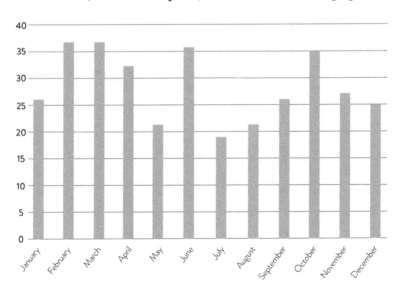

**Step 6:** Instantly, you'll see a full timeline that illustrates where your 'peak' proposal seasons occurred in each calendar year. While the peaks may vary somewhat, there will likely be a pattern that emerges. For instance, you may find that you experience peaks in late winter, early spring, midsummer, and early fall.

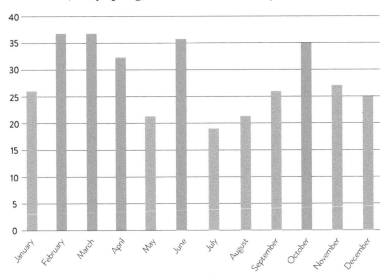

Now, you might already have a good inkling of when these seasons are, but seeing it in stark, visual terms allows you to train your eye on the months that are especially heavy with proposal work. It provides a loud punctuation mark that tells you: *These are not the times to plan big strategic projects.*

Once you have this visual marker of your reactive marketing, you will be ready to start incorporating your proactive marketing into an annual calendar. This chart will also come in handy when communicating with firm leadership about the timing of projects. It will serve as a major component of your story and one that will demonstrate your thoughtfulness and *awareness* of the forces that affect your marketing department's time and resources.

# CHAPTER TEN

# CREATING YOUR ANNUAL MARKETING CALENDAR

"We saw more demand for internal marketing over the last few years: working with
management to reduce turnover by supporting staff social events, creating an internal
newsletter, designing materials to nurture company culture. Seeing how much people
enjoyed these things, how eager they were for connection, made the work worthwhile, but it
took a lot of time. As an example, each issue of the monthly newsletter averaged 50 hours of
staff time, with the majority of that falling to me and the graphic designer."
Melissa C. (Marketing/Business Development professional, speaking about a former employer)

Now that you know when your typical proposal peaks occur,
you're ready to create a visual timeline of the year ahead.
Plot out the months and start by highlighting your busy seasons.
Then make note of other events, milestones, and marketing commitments. Regard your marketing calendar as a commandment.
Use it to chart weekly, monthly, quarterly, and annual tasks. Keep
these front and center to help you visualize when to take on new
internal projects and when to give yourself some slack. And be
sure to note vacations and personal milestones. Have a wedding
coming up? Acknowledge it! Moving into a new house or apart-
ment? Mark it down. Do you have a staffer who is gearing up for
parental leave? Make sure it's accounted for. Milestones in our
personal lives can affect our work lives, too. Embrace that and let
it inform your marketing strategy.

When shown to your firm leadership, it will be a powerful tool
in demonstrating thoughtful leadership. Your ability to capture
and command time is one of the most sought-after traits of a

marketing professional. Don't sell this step short for the impact it can have on firm confidence.

### ⏱ Timekeeper: 2-4 hours

**Step 1:** Gather your team and use a whiteboard, an online spreadsheet, or a simple piece of paper to draw a timeline that begins with January (or whatever month you want to start with) and plot out 12 months with hatch marks.

**Step 2:** Using different colors, start filling it out! First note when your proposal peaks typically occur (*see Chapter 9*). From there, note the holidays your firm recognizes, birthdays, and planned vacations. If you have significant milestones coming up like a wedding, a new baby, a graduation, and so forth, get it on there! We want to start creating a baseline for the major events that will happen throughout the year (and that includes what's happening in your personal life).[5]

**Step 3:** Note if there are any major firm events coming up—a senior staff retirement or a new office opening. Add in company events like all-staff retreats, company picnics, and holiday parties. Note major conferences and events with known dates.

**Step 4:** If you have major projects identified (a website overhaul, branding redesign, CRM restructuring, etc.) now is the time to review the calendar and determine when your team has capacity to work on it. Do you feel like your list of major projects is stagnant or incomplete? You will have time to review and refine it during your annual marketing retreat. *See Chapter 18 for more information.*

**Step 5:** Once you have all of your commitments present and accounted for—with time given to all marketing staff to weigh in—take this draft calendar and lay it out in a visually-appealing and coherent manner and share it with your firm leaders as part of your regular marketing report.

---

[5] Note: Only capture birthdays, personal events, and milestones for your marketing staff.

# Annual Marketing Calendar

| | JAN | FEB | MAR | APR | MAY | JUN | JUL | AUG | SEPT | OCT | NOV | DEC |
|---|---|---|---|---|---|---|---|---|---|---|---|---|
| Proposals | Proposal Peak | Proposal Peak | | | | Proposal Peak | | | | Proposal Peak | | |
| Reports | | Q4 Report | | Q1 Report | | | | Q2 Report | | | | Q3 Report |
| Events | Conference | | Conference | Conference | Conference | | | | | | | |
| Staff | | | Retirement | | | | | | Retirement | | | |
| Interns | | | | | | Summer Intern | Summer Intern | Summer Intern | | | | |
| Retreats | Management Retreat | | | | | | | | | | All-Staff Retreat | Marketing Retreat |
| Training | | | | Staff Training | | | | | Staff Training | | | |
| Initiatives | | | | | | Website Redesign | Website Redesign | Office Build-Out | Office Build-Out | | | |

CHAPTER ELEVEN

# IT TAKES A VILLAGE: DIALING IN STAFF ROLES AND RESPONSIBILITIES

*"We're not only chasing what's out there, we're also trying to stay strategic in what we're chasing. Having the time to have these meetings, having the time to be strategic is helping. We're cleaning up our file systems. We have time to do the work that until recently we've just been too busy to do." – Lindsay D. (Marketing Manager, architecture firm)*

Whether you are a department of one or many, getting your head wrapped around where your time goes throughout the day and how and *when* marketing activities take place is an essential fixture of a well-run marketing engine. Some of you wear all the hats, some of you are part of a larger marketing team. Each of you has finite time and several distinct (and sometimes competing) roles and obligations. Sitting down and reviewing the actual energy spent on those roles and obligations is an important annual discussion that will help reinforce the application and value of time.

A good starting point in creating a conversation around this is to review how last year went. Where *did* all that time go that wasn't spent working on proposals? By pulling and analyzing past time sheets[6], you can tease out proposal hours and compare that level-of-effort with the amount of time spent on other marketing activities.

---

[6] Note that this step will require coordination with your accounting department if you do not have easy access to past timesheets. The leader of your marketing team (typically your marketing director or manager) should collaborate with accounting to retrieve this data.

## ⏱ Timekeeper: 4-6 hours once you have the information at hand[7]

**Step 1:** Request a report—in Excel format—from Accounting (if you cannot pull this information yourself) for time billed in the last calendar year by each marketing staff member.

| SAMPLE TIMESHEET: AVERY SMITH, MARKETING MANAGER, 2019 HOURS ALLOCATION | | |
|---|---|---|
| Task: | Hours | Comment |
| Strategic Planning | 2 | Report creation for quarterly updates to Board |
| Strategic Planning | 1 | Budget analysis |
| Strategic Planning | 1 | Marketing Retreat refinement |
| Client Outreach | 2 | Mtgs: XYZ Consulting, ABC Engineering Group |
| Client Outreach | 1.5 | Client coffee catch-up |
| Client Outreach | 0.5 | LinkedIn follow-ups with teaming partners |
| Executive | 8 | Board retreat |
| Executive | 1 | Operations Committee |
| Executive | 1 | Quarterly Report presentation |
| Events | 1 | Conference prep |
| Events | 2.5 | Awards dinner |
| Events | 2.25 | Civic Annual Fundraiser Luncheon |
| Management | 2.5 | Training on Quals database |
| Management | 1 | Indd and resume template training |
| Management | 0.5 | Style training with editorial contractor |
| Marketing Administration | 6.5 | SO. MANY. LEADS. |
| Marketing Administration | 3 | Leads tracking, corralling Go/No-Gos |
| Marketing Administration | 2 | Marketing check in, leads tracking |
| Corporate Design | 0.75 | graphic updates |
| Corporate Design | 0.5 | color palette convo |
| Corporate Design | 3 | Test run and edits to new template design |
| Website Updates | 0.25 | Update office locations |
| Website Updates | 1 | Looking at analytics; fix spacing issue |
| Website Updates | 0.25 | New staff on website |

---

[7] Note that this task can take longer the first time you do it. As you continue to dial in your time codes, the process will become quicker and more efficient.

**Step 2:** Create a new spreadsheet titled "Marketing Staff Time Analysis" and create tabs for each individual, including yourself. Starting with your own tab, write down labels for the different types of activities that you regularly bill your time to.[8]

| SAMPLE ACTIVITY TALLY: AVERY SMITH, MARKETING MANAGER, 2019 HOURS ALLOCATION | | | | | |
|---|---|---|---|---|---|
| **Task:** | **Hours** | | | | |
| Proposals | | | | | |
| Marketing Administration | | | | | |
| Events | | | | | |
| Client Outreach | | | | | |
| Event Coordination | | | | | |
| Event Attendance | | | | | |
| Design Services | | | | | |
| Website Updates | | | | | |
| Social Media Postings | | | | | |
| Management | | | | | |
| Executive | | | | | |
| Strategic Planning | | | | | |
| Branding for New Office | | | | | |
| Newsletter | | | | | |
| | | | | | |
| | | | | | |
| | | | | | |
| | | | | | |
| Avery Smith | | Robin Garcia | | Austin Williams | |

[8] It's important to note that this will depend on what types of codes are currently configured in your company. Go into this assuming that the first year you perform this exercise the results will be incomplete and imperfect. You will likely discover that by simply adding in new time code categories, when you perform this analysis again a year from now you will find a richer, more accurate picture of marketing staff utilization.

**Step 3:** Now the work really begins! From here, you will need to dig into the data. Start by looking at proposals. Most firms have unique proposal codes for each pursuit. Proposal coordinators should be billing all time spent on proposals to these codes. Tally up the total number of hours dedicated to proposals and enter it on each staffer's individual tab.

**Step 4:** Continue through each staffer's time report and catalogue where they billed their time. For example, for marketing assistants, you may notice that the bulk of their non-proposal time is in Marketing Administration—this will be wholly unique per person.

| SAMPLE ACTIVITY TALLY: AVERY SMITH, MARKETING MANAGER, 2019 HOURS ALLOCATION | | | | | |
|---|---|---|---|---|---|
| Task: | Hours | | | | |
| Proposals | 418.25 | | | | |
| Marketing Administration | 352.5 | | | | |
| Events | 47 | | | | |
| Client Outreach | 170.75 | | | | |
| Event Coordination | 62 | | | | |
| Event Attendance | 102 | | | | |
| Design Services | 252.5 | | | | |
| Website Updates | 58.5 | | | | |
| Social Media Postings | 24.75 | | | | |
| Management | 95 | | | | |
| Executive | 129 | | | | |
| Strategic Planning | 52 | | | | |
| Branding for New Office | 44.5 | | | | |
| Newsletter | 98 | | | | |
| | 1906.75 | | | | |
| | | | | | |
| | | | | | |
| | | | | | |
| Avery Smith | | Robin Garcia | | Austin Williams | |

**Step 5:** Once you have each person's time tallied by code category, select the cells, click the chart tab and select the pie chart. Once the pie charts are created, you can right click on them and copy them as .jpegs into a Word document. Seeing them side-by-side, you will have your visual baseline for where everyone's time is going. And this information is *powerful*.

AVERY SMITH, MARKETING MANAGER, 2019 HOURS ALLOCATION

Once you can visualize where your time is *really* going, you can better control it. Look at these charts together as a group (this can happen in a special meeting or as part of your annual marketing retreat). *See Chapter 18.*

---

**Don't have the time codes you *really* need?** Identify what codes are relevant for your team and request that Accounting add them.

**Common codes:**

▶ Marketing Administration (Marketing Check-ins, data entry)

▶ Client Outreach (coffee check-ins, meet and greets, cold calls, etc.)

▶ Event Coordination

▶ Event Attendance

▶ Website Updates

▶ Design Services

▶ Strategic Planning (marketing retreat, activities covered in this book, marketing plan development, etc.)

▶ Management (coordination of interns and contractors, staff check-ins)

▶ Executive (meetings with firm leadership)

---

Where are your time sinks occurring? Where is the redundancy? What roles are languishing while others have too much time devoted to them? Discuss your current job titles and whether your time is truly dedicated to your core responsibilities. Is your marketing manager spending enough time managing? Is your business development lead spending too much time on proposals and not enough time out in the field? Is your team's time spent on the website and social media virtually non-existent? Discuss your observations as a group, own up to how you've handled (or mis-handled) your team's time.

The end-result of this conversation may lead to a startling conclusion: that staff time isn't well-utilized. This is great! You can't fix a problem that you don't know you have.

The truth is, our time is finite. All those increments add up to a hard number. Even when actively tracking time, you will eventually hit a wall when it comes to addressing and implementing certain projects. Marketing staff wage hard-earned battles for every part-time and full-time position. Our powers of persuasion on the ROI of internal marketing resources can only stretch so far. The overhead cost of each position weighs heavy on the minds of firm leadership who are juggling a list of competing cost demands.

When your firm's appetite for in-house talent acquisition has maxed out, it's time to turn their attention to lower-cost external 'release valves'. Accentuating your bench of in-house talent with a roster of external contractors and interns can be an invaluable addition to any A/E/C marketing department.

### Independent Contractors

Just as our clients seek independent consultants to help them complete their projects, marketing staff sometimes require special skillsets that they don't have in-house. Or they find that the demand for certain skillsets—like graphic design and editorial assistance—far outstrips in-house supply of these resources. By establishing relationships with freelancers, you create an on-call pipeline of talent that can fill in at a moment's notice to tackle work, especially during peak proposal times.

Whether it's graphic design, report layout, copyediting, or website maintenance, your local markets are teeming with skilled professionals ready to help. This is especially true during economic downturns when the job market is flooded with folks recently laid off from their firms. As we speak, there are marketing professionals throughout the country competing for a smaller pool of jobs. Many of these people would welcome the opportunity to freelance, which in turn expands their network and keeps their portfolios fresh.

Finding talent is simply a matter of asking around and doing search queries online. Research your talent pool, conduct interviews, and zero in on one or two candidates that have the skillset you're looking for. Start by tossing them smaller tasks to help ease them into your firm's particular way of conducting work. This will give them time to learn your file structures, nomenclature, and preferred methods of communication. Discuss and agree upon a fee structure that makes sense for your organization and work with your accounting department to determine how they would like to handle invoicing.

Discuss who on your team will manage your contractors. There should be one point-of-contact that oversees marketing requests that would be appropriate to outsource. This person is responsible for lining up time with the contractor and ensuring the work goes smoothly. This is a natural task for a marketing manager or a good skill-building exercise for a senior marketing coordinator.

---

**Securing permission from your firm leadership to utilize external help is a nuanced conversation.** You need to establish and explain the value proposition. If off-loading a 100-page editing project means more time spent honing your message and developing competitive proposals, the thought of paying for a few hours of a freelancer's time will be much more palatable. The same holds true when you consider the increase in demand for visually-appealing final deliverables. If a client is expecting a graphically-oriented final report, hiring a freelance graphic designer may result in a better work product than one cobbled together in-house amidst other competing deadlines.

Given that hourly rates of freelancers don't include the steep overhead costs of in-house staff, outsourcing certain project work versus hiring additional staff can make for a compelling argument. Also noteworthy: this could serve as an excellent opportunity to diversify your resources in terms of gender, ethnicity, and age.

---

# CHAPTER TWELVE

# THE CRITICAL VALUE OF INTERNS

"I've noticed a lot more emails coming in now of people trying to get my attention. We are frantically trying to get our offices the signage they need to address COVID-19, handling our owner's statements, and trying to respond meaningfully to the social justice movement. I feel like we're running around frantically trying to be helpful, but we're also trying to figure out what's going to happen next week. We're just inundated with requests and things to do." Christina B. (Assistant Vice President of Marketing, property management firm)

Most A/E/C firms have an established internship program. These not only expand their pool of affordable resources for project work, they also open up a pipeline for potential job candidates. Internship programs help shape future staff resources, establish networks to universities, and help encourage diversity in an industry where it is still sorely lacking. But with all the known benefits of this type of program, marketing internship programs are still a rarity.

Most marketing professionals in the A/E/C industry got their experience 'on the job' with few educational opportunities available in college curricula for this type of niche marketing. Knowing this, there is unlimited potential that can be unlocked by developing a marketing internship program. There are college students in a variety of majors developing knowledge in fields related to the work we do. Whether it's marketing and communications, English, journalism, or writing and book publishing programs—these students are learning about new technologies and applications that our firms need—and they are hungry for experience.

By utilizing interns, you can get out in front of non-proposal-related marketing projects that require time-consuming start-up tasks—tasks that often fall by the wayside, leading to stalled projects and frustrated technical staff. This constant one step forward, two steps back degrades the focus and efficiency of your marketing staff and can demoralize your team by breeding stress that 'things are just not getting done'.

The list of projects an intern can work on is limited only by your imagination. Common tasks include staff resume updates, proofreading, market research, competitor evaluations, social media audits (*see Chapter 15*), website analytics, and conference and award research. While unpaid internships exist, offering a small hourly wage—minimum wage or slightly higher—will generate a lot of interest.

Interns, typically students, are eager to work! They are conditioned to perform based on a grading system and see internships as an extension of their education. They are unburdened by the pressures of day-to-day office life and are able to focus solely on the task at hand. An intern making $15 an hour, working 12 hours a week for 10 weeks will cost your company $1,800. To put that in perspective, a 'bronze' or 'silver' sponsorship typically costs between $1,500 and $2,000 and buys you—at most—1 or 2 days of brand exposure. The value of an internship far outpaces this in terms of return on investment. Indeed, what an intern can do in 10 weeks of focused, concentrated time, can take a salaried marketing coordinator twice as long—all with an opportunity cost of lost time on the other myriad projects and proposals constantly in flux.

"My time has become over-obligated and I'm having to work nights and weekends just to do the front-end work." – Anonymous

## ⏱ Timekeeper: 4-8 hours

**Step 1:** Review your list of special projects for the calendar year and identify the tasks most suited for your intern.

**Step 2:** Determine the estimated hours needed to complete each task and the technology needed. (At minimum, your intern will need a laptop, a workstation, a company-assigned email address, and access to file systems. You may also need to establish permissions and passwords for online accounts and access to the back-end of your website.)

**Step 3:** Draft a job description and determine the hourly rate your firm is willing to pay.

**Step 4:** Post your job announcement on your website, at local universities, and other online job-search portals.

**Step 5:** Establish a hiring committee and discuss the traits you want in an intern.

**Step 6:** Once you have selected your intern, determine who will manage their time. During onboarding, discuss the tasks you would like them to complete and schedule regular check-ins to track their progress.

**Step 7:** Plan on giving periodic reports to your firm leadership on the outcomes and deliverables that the intern is working on, and make to sure to note how their work is helping you meet your strategic goals.

**Step 8:** Breathe a sigh of relief as you focus on the core tenants of your job, knowing that the foundational work of your strategic projects is getting done!

**Sample Intern Task List**

▶ Resume updates and formatting in Word and InDesign templates

▶ Project description consolidation

▶ Track down boilerplate (text that can be re-used/re-purposed for proposals and website)

▶ Website analytics (unique visitors, most frequently visited pages, time spent on site, if they found the site by search engine, etc.)

▶ 'Info' Scout (outreach to staff and project folder research to track down and capture obscure information: project start and end dates, construction costs, contract numbers, etc.)

▶ Upcoming conferences and events research

▶ Social media audits

▶ Competitor evaluations

▶ Client funding and grant cycle research

▶ Awards applications

▶ Swag/tchotchke vendor and pricing research

▶ Online firm identity/branding research (investigate website 'discovery' in search engine queries, review staff feedback reviews on Glassdoor, search for news and other media mentions, etc.)

# CHAPTER THIRTEEN

# TIGHTEN UP LEADS TRACKING

*"They are now taking on pursuits that they normally wouldn't have gone after, which is causing our hit rate to fall. In some cases, we're not even hearing back on these bids, which compels me to spend a lot of time on the phone following up."*
Anonymous

Now on to another important—but often overlooked—facet of your day-to-day: leads tracking. How many times have you heard those frustrated comments: "How did we miss this?!" "Why did I have to learn about this lead from a teaming partner?" "We should have seen this when it came out two weeks ago!" These statements send a chill down the spine of a marketing coordinator. How *did* you miss it? You track leads every day ... how did *this* one slip past you?

This is a cloudy question and one you probably spend a nominal amount of time trying to answer. You typically search old emails and check your filters for a few minutes before your attention is inevitably drawn to more pressing matters: that proposal deadline, that interview prep, that client meeting. But that cloudy question remains. And every lead that is missed erodes staff confidence that Marketing is 'on top of things'.

While you *can't* 100% avoid the occasional lost lead, a once-annual review of your leads tracking process will allow you to tighten the bolts, review your key words, add new ones, and consider new vendors. Make this review transparent. Invite staff to ask questions. Circulate the leads tracking keywords to staff for their review. Give a brief presentation on how leads are tracked at your next staff meeting. This kind of inclusion and transparency breeds confidence in your methods and lets your firm leadership know that you are doing your diligent best to ensure that every viable lead is captured.

Because marketing departments experience a fairly high rate of turnover, you may be using a system, a vendor, or a process that was created by a predecessor. This is a foundational component of your marketing engine and one that you must wholly own and command. There are several questions to wrap your head around. By taking the time ask these questions, you will ensure an environment where your team feels best able to monitor the very life-blood of your organization—new projects!

### ⏲ Timekeeper: 4-6 hours total, including meetings

**Step 1: Review your master list.** Are all of your leads tracking vendors and individual agency websites captured in one master list? If not, create it! This list should include the name of each vendor or agency, usernames, passwords, and the email address where the lead notifications are sent. (Use an online spreadsheet that is easy to update and share.) Consider making this list available to all staff, so they understand the breadth of surveillance required to track leads.

**Step 2: What's missing?** Invite staff to review the list and make suggestions for City, County, and State portals that they want added to the list. During recessions, technical staff may begin turning their attention to new marketplaces. Know where they are hunting for work and create accounts with new agencies, so you are ready at a moment's notice to track those leads.

**Step 3: Review your list of key words.** Do you have a master list of key words for each of your service areas? If you don't, create one!

This list is not only vital when setting up filters on vendor websites, it serves as an excellent primer for new marketing staff who are still getting acquainted with the types of work you do. Knowing these key words backward and forward trains your eye to quickly shuffle through a new batch of incoming leads—dismissing leads that aren't relevant to your organization and zeroing in on the ones that are.

**Step 4: Cross-train your marketing staff.** Most marketing departments typically have one staffer who is responsible for tracking leads (or one staffer per service area in very large firms). What happens when your leads tracker takes a vacation, calls in sick, or moves on to another firm? You can't just press the pause button when this happens. Those leads will keep coming in! By training all of your marketing staff on how to track leads you ensure a seamless system where someone is always mentally ready to pick up this task when needed. Set aside time in your marketing check-in for this. Special one-off trainings may also be valuable. State agency procurement websites and Beta.Sam.gov (formerly known as FedBizOpps.gov) are complex and confusing to new users. Make sure your entire team is familiar enough with them to not simply get lost in the details when trying to track down an important lead.

**Step 5: Review how leads are distributed.** What happens when a viable lead comes in? Who is it sent to for review and Go/No-Go conversations? How do you track which leads are converted to proposals and which get tossed? How do you ensure that your firm is reviewing and Go-ing leads in a timely manner? If you regularly find that leads languish for too long or that you don't have the right mix of technical staff reviewing them, review your bottlenecks and refine your system. Again, creating an online, sharable spreadsheet is an excellent low-cost way to capture all incoming leads and track their progress through your pipeline. If you use a CRM system to distribute leads, review its efficiency.

**Step 6: Reinvigorate your relationship with your vendors.** There are many for-profit leads-tracking vendors that cater to the A/E/C industry. GovWin, IMS, and Salesforce are commonly known, but there are others on the market, as well. Paying for this type of service can greatly decrease the amount of time you spend tracking leads, but they are not perfect. If you find that you are getting a lot of 'chaff' mixed in with the 'wheat', it's time to make a call to your assigned representative and review your filters. You're paying for these services. Make sure you're getting the most out them!

# CHAPTER FOURTEEN

# THE CLIENT SURVEY

*"A lot of people think clients don't want to be bothered, but we're all isolated.*
*People welcome the opportunity to talk."*
Bonnie T. (Strategic Pursuit Manager, environmental/water engineering firm)

Now let's move outward. How are your clients doing? How do they feel about your products? How do they feel about your report writing? Did your work help them accomplish the goals of their project? Would they work with you again?

Marketing is often one step removed from the clients. We engage them on the front end, but detach once the project is won. What we forget is that the marketing of our services does not end the moment we win the project. That subtle touch of reaching out and saying "How did we do?" provides an invaluable opportunity to connect with our clients in a meaningful and important way.

Occasionally we'll get called in by technical staff to debrief with a client, but these requests are typically random and only geared toward top-shelf clients. All clients deserve our outreach and attention. But in the hustle and bustle of everyday work, this type of follow-up tends to fall by the wayside. So how do you build in time for it without pulling your attention away from everything else? The answer is a mix of automation and streamlined outreach.

## Automating Client Outreach

Many firms employ an integrated CRM system that connects project work with accounting and invoicing. It is not uncommon that automated emails go out to relevant staff notifying them when a project is closed. Check with your accounting department to see if it is possible to have these notices sent to an assigned point-of-contact in Marketing.[9] When an email comes in that a project has officially ended, this provides an opportunity to follow up with the project lead. Let them know that you are ready to deploy the client survey, ask them who is the best contact to send it to, and get their sign-off on sending it. On occasion, there may be a reason not to send it. Sometimes the work is ongoing, or your part of the project was buried within a multidisciplinary team. Sometimes the project manager knows that the project did not go well, and they are fearful of what the feedback might be and how that will reflect on them. It's important to give the staffer the opportunity to voice that. You want to build trust with your staff that ultimately, you are on their side—that the purpose of this information is to work toward continued improvement, not to malign or harm your technical staffs' reputations or standing within your firm.

Once you have your list of approved clients, you need to decide on timing of the deployment. You don't want too much time to pass between when the project ended and when they receive the survey. But you also don't want to constantly stop what you're working on to send them out. Deploying the survey on a quarterly basis allows you to block off a set amount of time to focus on the task and ensures that the survey goes out in a window when your client's recollection of the project work will still be relatively fresh.

---

[9] Before contacting your accounting department, be sure you get buy-in from your supervisor and other decision-makers in the firm. You don't want to get sideways of your firm leadership when interacting with your client base. Set up a meeting to discuss. Perhaps send them this chapter to read!

**Negative feedback is also valuable.** It allows you to identify relationships that are in jeopardy.

"I received feedback from a client who had been contracting work to us for years. She said that she was disappointed in the most recent report and that she wasn't happy that much of the work had been delegated to a junior staffer who wasn't as well-versed in client relations. However, she made note that she appreciated being asked and that if she hadn't received the survey she likely wouldn't have felt inclined to reach out. Instead she would have very likely just hired another firm for her next project. After reviewing her feedback, the president of the company personally called her to discuss the situation, offered to make it right, and by the end of the conversation the relationship was repaired and back on track." - Anonymous

There are several low-cost or no-cost online services you can use that provide customizable templates. For instance, SurveyMonkey provides a free service for surveys of 10 questions or less. (And 10 questions are plenty!) Make it as quick and easy to fill in as possible. The easier it is, the more responses you'll get.

Pick your top burning questions and make some of the fields optional and some mandatory. Asking a small assortment of focused questions accomplishes several things. You get helpful feedback that can guide improvements in your work products, you will accumulate comments directed at staff members that will either serve as a nice shot in the arm for a job well done or as constructive feedback to help with performance improvements. Additionally, if the client is extremely happy with the work, you know who to put on the short list for client appreciation gifts, invites to company events, and other personal touches to further solidify in their mind that you are the ONLY firm they think of when they think of your services.

## ⏱ Timekeeper: 2-4 hours

**Step 1**: Research online survey vendors and select which one you want to use.

**Step 2:** Create your account and build out a template for your questions. Here is a simple and effective list:

1. Name (Optional)

2. Title of Project (Optional)

3. Names of Staff You Worked With (Optional)

4. Overall Quality of the Work (dropdown: Excellent, Good, Average, Poor, Very Poor)

5. Were Your Phone Calls and Emails Responded to in a Timely Fashion? (dropdown: Yes, No)

6. Was the Quality of the Work Products: (include a series of dropdowns nested under this question)

    a. Technically Rigorous

    b. Well Written

    c. Grammatically Clean and Free of Typos

    d. Visually Appealing

7. Did our work help you achieve the goals of your project? (dropdown: Yes, No)

8. Was the project completed on time and on budget? (dropdown: Yes, No)

9. Would you work with our firm again? (dropdown: Yes, No)

10. Additional comments (open field)[10]

---

[10] This field is particularly useful as it allows them an opportunity to clarify their answers. For answers that are especially complimentary, you can follow up and request permission to use them as testimonials!

**Step 3:** Draft up a boilerplate email message that you can tailor with the client's contact name and the name of the project. This should be a brief email that lets them know you heard the project was recently completed and that feedback on staff performance is extremely valuable to your company. Include a link to the survey and ask them to fill it out, noting that it was designed to be a very quick process. Save this boilerplate to use in tailored emails when you deploy your survey.

**Step 4:** You will receive notices when clients have taken the survey. Review the results and send them to relevant staff, such as the project principal and manager and a designated member of your leadership team. This could be the company's CEO or president, the COO, or other firm leaders who want to be kept informed about project performance.

Over time, you will accumulate a treasure trove of client feedback. Adding this component to your marketing engine provides a relatively low effort, high-yield activity that produces rich data to inform your business development strategies. And it is yet another opportunity to maintain and nurture your ownership's trust that you are truly the sentinels of your company's brand.

# CHAPTER FIFTEEN

# DIGITAL MARKETING:
# REACH YOUR AUDIENCE WITHOUT
# WASTING YOUR TIME

*"The world is not the same as it was at the beginning of this year. We're using social media a lot more to not only promote our work, but also what we stand for."*
Angie C. (Marketing Director, construction firm)

We live in the digital age and much of our day is spent (for better or worse) on our smartphones or tied to our computers. We've all been swept up with the social media fever for more than a decade, but this is still an emerging marketing platform and one that many of us have had to learn how to use on the fly. When the pandemic, economic shutdown, and social justice movement took hold in early 2020, we found ourselves relying more heavily on social media to stay connected and to communicate our company responses to the overwhelming change and culture conversations happening across the country. This has caused more firms to invest time and resources into their online presence, but understanding just how *much* time and energy to commit to social media is difficult to quantify.

The vast majority of A/E/C firms have some sort of social media plan in place. Most marketing professionals are convinced of the power and opportunity to be had or lost by embracing or not embracing the social media doctrine. But in the quest to reach our audiences online, we often overreach—creating profiles on more platforms than we can realistically manage. We go in with great expectations—dreaming up the content we'll produce and the reactions it will inspire, only to develop long gaps of radio silence between postings. We spend significant amounts of time coordinating (cajoling, pestering, hounding) technical staff to feed us interesting information about recent projects, but may only have a small number of followers who will see it (and fewer still who will like, share, or comment on it).

Oftentimes we receive pressure from firm leadership who spot interesting posts in their own social media feeds. They covet the idea of generating online content but don't have a clear sense of the time it takes to do it right or at what volume to produce it as compared to our competitors.

And competition is one of the main motivations that drives social media. We engage always with the knowledge that our competition is *also* out there in the online realm. Are they beating us in the social media game? Are they building their brand while we fumble on our implementation? What kind of following do they have? Are clients and teaming partners following their every move? What exactly *are* they doing?

Now is the time to take a long, critical look at how your firm *truly* stacks up against your competition. You do this by conducting a social media 'audit'. This is a perfect task for an intern and one that could greatly inform your social media strategy and level of effort.

🕐 **Timekeeper: 6-8 hours**

**Step 1:** Start by creating a list of your top competitors and teaming partners, as well as firms you aspire to work with.

**Step 2:** Create a simple spreadsheet to capture metrics, including:

a. List of platforms they are active on (typically LinkedIn, Twitter, Facebook, and sometimes Instagram)

b. Frequency of posts (daily, weekly, monthly, erratic—be sure to note any large gaps, as well as the date of their most recent post)

c. Type of content (project spotlights, new staff announcements, awards, articles, firm culture statements, reposts of compelling industry news, etc.)

d. Note if their content is identical across platforms (followers often tune out when they start noticing a 'synthetic' quality to an organization's online content)

e. Number of followers per platform

Once you have this data in-hand, ask yourself some hard questions: are they creating a genuine presence via these platforms or just adding to the background noise. Do you *need* to compete on each of these platforms or is your time and energy better spent on one in particular? The activities of your competitors should shine a light on your own. Ask yourself if all the hard work is worth it if your Twitter account is only producing a few retweets and likes per posting. Be honest, is Facebook an appropriate platform to effectively market your services if the majority of followers are your own staff?

Now that we have had a decade to get used to this new role of digital marketing, it's time to make discerning, strategic decisions about how we harness it. Otherwise, we're just spinning our wheels with little or no return on this time investment.

Example of a Real Social Media Audit

| FIRMS TO REVIEW | FB: # OF POSTS | FB: CONTENT | TWITTER: # OF POSTS | TWITTER: CONTENT | LINKEDIN: # OF POSTS | LINKEDIN: CONTENT |
|---|---|---|---|---|---|---|
| "Firm 1" | Erratic, not often; once/ month or less; 264 followers | Same as content on LinkedIn and Twitter; not much of it but nice pictures | Erratic, not often; once/ month or less; 264 followers | Mostly same as LinkedIn | Erratic, not often; once/ month or less; 1,663 followers | Awards won, high-profile proposals, employees |
| "Firm 2" | 1-4 times/ month; 187 followers | Mostly share articles about their projects; some about conferences; some about awards won | A little bit more often– 5-10 times/ month; 375 followers | Same articles shared on FB | 1-2 times/ month or less; 765 followers | Some of the same articles shared on FB and Twitter |
| "Firm 3" | Very inconsistent, only 2 posts in 2019; 179 followers | More consistent in 2020; shared drone aerial images, projects working on, awards won, relevant articles | Same as FB; 156 followers | Same as FB | No posts; 90 followers | None |
| "Firm 4" | About once/ month; 189 followers | More staff-focused, share pictures of what's going on at their office, projects they're working on; also show community engagement | Same as FB, about once/ month, 39 followers | Same as FB | No posts; 175 followers | None |
| "Firm 5" | Almost daily; 20,491 followers | Share industry news, pictures of their projects; pictures of staff party | Same as FB; 4,640 followers | Mostly the same as what's shared on FB; use hashtags and tagging well | Same; 15,413 followers | Same as shared on others |
| "Firm 6" | 1-3 times/ week; 911 followers | Share relevant articles about them and their projects, look into their new office | Sometimes multiple times a day, 962 followers | Updates on projects, use hashtags like #architecture, share quotes from linked articles | About the same as FB; 2,634 followers | Mostly same as FB content |
| "Firm 7" | Almost daily; 23,343 followers | Information on projects, industry news, graphics and videos | Daily or multiple times a day; 50.3K followers | Use hashtags, same industry news as FB | Almost daily; 366,383 followers | Same as FB |

# CHAPTER SIXTEEN

# ESTABLISH (OR REFINE)
# YOUR MARKETING BUDGET

"I feel like I really need to justify all expenses coming out of Marketing now.
I have definitely put more pressure on myself to spend more wisely."
Kelsey P. (Marketing Manager, engineering firm)

Now on to a really tricky, but important one. As nonsensical as it sounds, many A/E/C companies do not have a determined set-aside marketing budget, beyond having a billing code or two to monitor marketing-related activities. There are several compelling reasons to empower a marketing department with a true budget. Your staff attend events and conferences and hopefully speak at them. How many times have they come to you saying "Maybe we should sponsor this." How many times have you learned after the fact that some decision maker at your firm committed you to a sponsorship without telling you until the last minute? Sponsorships, combined with philanthropic giving (buying tables for worthy, related events, donating services or volunteering staff hours to causes) increase exposure, get you closer to your clients and teaming partners, and show that you truly care about your industry and community partners.

In addition to that, another cost point that routinely goes untracked is staff memberships. Many companies gladly foot the bill for technical staff memberships to relevant organizations. We often see these listed on staff resumes. But beyond having the membership, are they involved? Are they attending events and serving on committees? Membership to industry organizations provide excellent opportunities to network and show brand loyalty to the organization, but if your staff aren't attending the events, the cost of the membership merely translates to a line item on their resume.

The first step is to corral a master list of all staff memberships. A simple email to each technical staffer will get you close to the final tally. Ask them to list all memberships that they have and if the company pays for them. (They may be floating the cost of their own memberships and this is important to note as well.)

Once you have the information in hand, it's time to start thinking through a list of expectations for memberships paid for by your firm. This could include a request that staff attend at least two events a year, serve on a committee, attend the annual conference, or actively look for ways to submit papers or session applications. You may decide to cap the number of memberships for a given organization. (If you have a large number of staff who have memberships, but only a handful who are actively using them, it may be worth considering the overall value that those commitments bring to your firm.)

Having the master list—knowing what the true cost of all these memberships are—gives you a dollar amount that you can then look at with a critical eye. While Marketing isn't typically the final word on who has a membership and who doesn't, these are marketing dollars and should be factored into your overall budget. Once you capture this cost, you will have an easier time of making the case for other types of expenditures. "We spend X on network marketing. To compliment that we should consider Y."

For instance, you may consider ad placements. Local public radio is typically geared to issues that your clients and teaming partners track closely. Consider an ad placement that occurs during the active session for your local legislature—when they will be commuting daily to the capital. "This programming is brought to you by...." can brand your firm to the issues and orient you in the minds of the very people you are trying to secure work with. This type of ad placement comes at a cost and typically requires buy-off from firm leadership. If you can proactively show that you know where every marketing dollar is going and can demonstrate the value of the placement as it relates to your overall budget you will have an easier time instilling confidence that you are making sound financial investments on behalf of the firm.

Have you been trying to break in with the media? Can't get the local industry journal to return your calls? Paying for seats at their events or sponsoring something now and then will greatly increase the likelihood of that happening. In order to create a healthy relationship where media consider you as experts to call upon, you have to be present and accounted for—playing an active and visible role in local events and discussions. You can't expect an enterprise of any sort to invest in you until you demonstrate that you are invested in them.

For those of you who serve as directors or the head of your marketing department, if you don't currently have a defined budget, now is the time to negotiate and advocate for one. Demonstrate your knowledge by cataloging where money is already being spent, then show how you could use it more efficiently and effectively. This can be a touchy subject, as owners are loathe to hand over any financial control to people outside the ownership pool and the upper echelons of management. But it's critical to establishing and testing that trust you're working so hard to cultivate. Convincing your leadership to hand over some of their spending power will solidify the notion that Marketing can thoughtfully allocate and spend money wisely. This may seem small but the symbolism is huge.

If you already have a set budget, now is the time to examine it. In recessions, firms often look to 'overhead' expenses first when making cuts. Marketing dollars tend to fall into this category for better or worse. Getting out in front of this and scrutinizing your spending before the owners do demonstrates that you are fiscally responsible and proactively looking for ways to maximize your dollars at a time when the value of each dollar spent means more. It also gives you a leg to stand on when you see signs that firm leadership are considering completely moth-balling a certain type of expense. For instance, the data shows that corporate gift giving is one of the first cuts made when times get tight.[11] But is this the right move? If *everybody* is cutting this type of spending, then you may have a greater share of exposure and heightened impact if you continue on in some fashion. By dialing down expenses across the board, you may be able to preserve certain marketing opportunities that other firms may shutter completely.

---

**Common Marketing Expenditures**
- Proposals
- Corporate gift giving
- Staff memberships
- Conference attendance (admission, travel, and lodging)
- Booths (sign-up fees and collateral costs)
- Sponsorships
- Ad placements
- Swag
- Philanthropic giving
- Event planning

---

[11] Refer to page 7 for a breakdown of cost-cutting measures taken in the Great Recession.

# CHAPTER SEVENTEEN

# CREATE TRANSPARENCY IN YOUR MARKETING TASKS

*"Our personal lives are important. We have to set boundaries and expectations from the beginning. I have worked overtime, but I don't want it to be the norm. We found that when we planned carefully and set those expectations, were still able to get everything done and we weren't killing ourselves. When you work smart, you can work better."*
Lindsay D. (Marketing Manager, architecture firm)

The marketing department is the 'oyster bed' of the organization. All manner of requests filter through the team—proposal support, leads tracking, graphic design, editorial, newsletter write-ups, tracking down imagery, research, website updates, and on and on. But there are many facets to what we do and more often than not, staff sometimes only view what we do from the vantage point of the facet most relevant to them. We are usually 'known' for one or two particular services that a given staff member relies on. And each staffer expects us to be ready and available when they have a request.

Saying 'No' or 'I don't have capacity' can corrode our relationships with staff who need on our services to do their jobs. In worst-case scenarios they simply give up and stop coming to us for help, which can divert marketing-related activities to non-marketing staff. To avoid this, we must educate our technical staff to the full spectrum of work we do day in and day out.

When working in an office setting, where people mill in and out of our office space, there is ample opportunity to 'market' the work we do. Go "analog" and put your ongoing schedule up where everyone can see it. A simple whiteboard with a large 2-month calendar located in a highly-trafficked area will say more to your fellow staffers than you trying to describe all of the various tasks your team is working on. Choose a place where your team can gather once a week to talk through triage, PTO, upcoming proposals, special projects, and potential roadblocks.

Chart out your workload in color-assigned buckets and note when they occur over the course of the coming weeks. Note upcoming proposals and who is assigned to each. Include upcoming events and client meetings. Let them see how BUSY you are. Instead of constantly defending yourself and all of the deadlines you're wrestling with, let the calendar speak for you. When project managers come to you with a short-fuse deadline and see that there are already two proposals due out that day, layout work piling up, and an event to prep for, they may think twice, or at the very least, work hard to make it easy on you. You may even find technical staffers wandering over to the calendar to quietly review it—looking for the best time to make their request!

**Calendar Categories**
- ▶ Proposals (priming) – red
- ▶ Proposals (subbing) – green
- ▶ Graphic design and editorial - pink
- ▶ In-house all-staff events and meetings – orange
- ▶ Business development activities (teaming partner meetings, calls and emails, coffee check-ins) – blue
- ▶ Events and conferences – brown
- ▶ Special projects and intern tasks – black
- ▶ Personal commitments - purple

Providing non-marketing staff with the full picture is the epitome of transparency and one that will breed recognition and respect for the hard work you do every day.

It may seem like a time-consuming process to keep a calendar like this updated, but when incorporated into your weekly or bi-weekly check-in it actually creates efficiency in assigning tasks because you can readily visualize staff assignments. For instance, if one coordinator has two proposals due toward the end of the month and another comes in the door that's due at the same time, you know you'll need to assign it to someone else!

Creating a visualization of your workload, across all team members will bring you closer together. You will respect each person's time in a holistic way—seeing how they fit into the whole group. Working as a team to track your workloads is the very foundation of the philosophy that you are 'all in this together'.

---

**How to be Transparent When Working Remotely**

The pandemic and shutdown of early 2020 compelled all of us to shift our work out of the office and into our homes. This may have long-term implications on where and how we do our work—likely opening the door to permanent hybrids where staff can choose to flex their time. If you still find your team predominately working remotely, make your calendar virtual. A simple online, sharable spreadsheet is a no-cost, easy-to-use option that can be shared company-wide (with editing restrictions put in place so only your team can update it).

---

CHAPTER EIGHTEEN

# RETREAT!

"It helps immensely that we respect each other. There's trust. We want to do well because we appreciate each other. Having the time to talk and know each other as individuals means we work hard to help each other balance our workloads. I know they'll help me out and I want to help them out. In the day-to-day it's easy to overlook how important that is."
Lindsay D. (Marketing Manager, architecture firm)

Your firm likely has an annual all-staff retreat that brings together folks from across the firm, removing them from the day-to-day to look at the bigger picture in a collaborative environment. It allows staff a chance to reflect on operations, strategy, and efficiencies. It's an important team-building exercise and one that helps create a shared vision for the year ahead.

If you think about it in terms of a battle, 'retreating' from the front line gives you a chance to regroup, reorganize, rest, and recharge. Battle fatigue wears down your resources and weakens your ability to 'fight'. This is true of your marketing staff as well. The pressures of shifting deadlines and triaging incoming work can cause us to unknowingly drift from the larger, broader context of how the work we do on any given day fits into the bigger picture of our marketing and business development strategies.

If your firm does not currently allow for a marketing retreat, now is the time to advocate for it. Emphasize that this will be a day to review your progress on special projects and to prioritize the implementation of new ones. Frame it as a chance to review and improve efficiencies. Let them know that you will be discussing staff roles and how to ensure that every staffer's time is being maximized *for the benefit of the firm.*

> **You may be met with resistance at first.** You may have decision-makers who are hesitant to pull all marketing resources at once. Let them know that the ultimate ROI of a Marketing Staff Retreat is to provide an even greater level of service. And remember, you're a marketing professional because you are good at selling! This is your chance to 'sell' your firm on this concept. So roll up your sleeves and be prepared to communicate and win them over.

Once you've secured the support of your firm leadership, it's time to set the date. Pick a day at least two months out. Choosing a Friday typically works best, as they tend to be 'quieter' in terms of new requests. This is important because when you retreat, you go *completely* radio silent. This means no proposals, no email responses, no phone calls, nothing. Just you, your team, your agenda, a computer to take notes, a stack of thank-you cards (yes, thank-you cards!) and loads of space to whiteboard and document your conversations. You go dark for one day, so you can come back roaring the following week.

Once you have the date set (earmark at least 6 to 8 hours for your retreat), sit down as a group and brainstorm your agenda.[12] At a minimum you should: review where your team's hours went in the last year, discuss your Annual Marketing Calendar, conduct a SWTO analysis (that is not a typo), and begin building the list of new projects that you want to prioritize in the coming year.

This is the time to talk about the bottlenecks and opportunities. Where you can express yourself in a safe space, reconnect, and acknowledge each other's important contributions to your firm.

---

[12] You will want to designate a facilitator (typically your Marketing Director or Manager) as well as a time-keeper who will ensure that you keep to your schedule.

It is also the time to talk about all of the great data and findings of the previous exercises discussed in this book. Looking at all of it in concert will serve as a compass as you map out the year ahead.

To kick off your retreat, build in 15 minutes for gratitude. It's easy to naturally gravitate to the things that 'aren't working', but take a moment to center yourselves around what is working. Give each person a minute or two to talk about what they are grateful for that morning. Take a moment to acknowledge your gratitude for each other. Immerse yourself in the moment and kick off your retreat with positive energy.

Next, transition into the first important discussion: Your individual roles and where your time was invested in the past year.

### Staff Time Review

As prep work leading up to the retreat, print out the pie charts discussed in Chapter 11. Print each in color on 8.5 x 11 inch pieces of paper so they are visible from across the room. Paste these to a large poster board and display them on an easel or affixed to a wall. You want this up for the duration of the retreat so each individual can glance at it and reflect on it over the course of the day.

Your facilitator for this discussion should be the leader of your group—either your director or manager. The facilitator should stand up next to the pie charts and discuss each one, pointing out where the majority of time was allocated, note any areas of overlap with other staffers, and note any areas that seem underdeveloped. Focus the discussion not only around how time should be allocated as it relates to their individual job descriptions, but also with a eye toward professional development. This is the chance to ask:

▸ "What did you enjoy working on the most in the last year?"

▸ "Where do you wish you had devoted more of your time?"

▸ "What work do you want to be doing? What isn't currently represented on your pie chart?"

This is the chance to tease out the hopes and dreams of your staff. Who wishes they had more time to help with event planning or market research? Who wants a greater role in leads tracking or proposal coordination? Having this conversation as a group pulls the whole team together to think of ways to support each other in reaching your individual professional goals. "Well, if I took on 10% more proposal work, that could free you up to work on our social media engagement strategy." "If I could get some help on next year's event planning, it could free me up to work on our in-house style guide."

You may also hear staff wishing out loud they want to be helpful in new ways, but know they need more training to do that. Talk about how you could build in time for training in the coming year. (It could focus on graphic design, CRM software, website maintenance or a host of other topics.) Discuss what kind of training your team wants and commit to building in time for it.

When given the chance, people yearn to help. When it is reciprocated, the bonds grow stronger. Just this activity alone will strengthen your team and renew your commitments and focus. Done as part of a retreat, it sets the stage for robust and collaborative discussions on every other agenda item. So don't skip it!

### Storyboard your Annual Marketing Calendar

Now is the time to clear out the cobwebs. You've already gone through the exercise of creating this calendar (*see Chapter 10*). Now it's time to do it again as part of your retreat!

Start by picking a wall that has ample room and tape up a roll of butcher paper or large pieces of poster paper. It should be no less than 5 feet long (and longer is even better if you can swing it). Using a black marker—and with a steady hand!—draw a timeline that begins with January (or whatever month you want to start with) and plot out 12 months with hatch marks. Using different colored markers, start filling it out. First note when your proposal peaks typically occur (*see Chapter 9*). From there, note the holidays your firm recognizes, birthdays, and planned vacations. If you have significant milestones coming up like a wedding, a new baby, a graduation, and so forth, get it on there! We want to create a baseline for the major events that will happen throughout the year (and that includes what's happening in your personal life).

Next, note if there are any major firm events coming up—a senior staff retirement or a new office opening. Add in company events like all-staff retreats, company picnics, and holiday parties. Note major conferences and events with known dates.

Once you've documented all milestones, busy seasons, and events take a step back as a group and assess how the year is shaping up. Take note of the times of year that are 'quieter'—these will be the times when you want to schedule the major activities on the priority list you'll develop later in the retreat.

## How to Conduct a Worthwhile SWTO Analysis[13]

Most of us in the A/E/C industry have taken part in a SWOT exercise at some point. But consider revising the order of these topics. Instead of concluding this invaluable analysis by fixating on Threats, use all of the insight and observations you have accumulated to inform your Opportunities—this is, after all—the most important outcome of the exercise. Engaging in a SWTO ('swato') may seem daunting at first, but with a few simple tactics you can elicit candid feedback that will help uncover inefficiencies, barriers, and bottlenecks occurring within your team. Re-emphasize that this is a safe space and that the outcomes of the SWTO will stay within your group. This component of the retreat is for you and you alone. Knowing that this information won't make its way back to the firm leadership will help ensure that all observations, frustrations, and critiques make their way into it.

To begin, you will need a small set of supplies: four poster-sized pieces of paper that you can affix to the wall, several sets of 3x3 inch Post-it pads in blue, green, pink, and orange (one for each category of the SWTO), and a black sharpie for each team member.

### ■ Strengths

With everyone seated around the table, pass out the blue Post-its and prompt the group to get them brainstorming. Ask several questions to orient the team around the topic. What makes our team special? What skills do we have? What is it about the way we run our department that sets us apart from others? What makes our company special? What is important about the work we do?

Using up to 10-15 minutes, have everyone jot down their ideas—one per Post-it—and have them stick them to the Strengths poster paper as they create them. Others in the group will be reviewing

---

[13] This exercise seems simple on the surface, but it ends up taking a lot of time (and it should)! Budget no less than 2 hours for this, ideally more. Every member of the team (including your facilitator and timekeeper) will take part in this exercise. To ensure that you stay on track, set an alarm for each brainstorming portion of the SWTO analysis.

notes that make it onto the board, which will spur further ideas. You'll be amazed at how many Post-its will be stuck up there in such a short amount of time!

As time is wrapping up, the facilitator will review the Post-its and start sorting them into common themes. You often find that multiple people write essentially the same thing down. Maybe you're all extremely proud of your proposal process, or you know that you have strong InDesign skills amongst your staff. As you start grouping the Post-its together, themes will begin to emerge. The groups that have a lot of Post-its are your greatest strengths. (You may even find team members writing a strength down again, just to reiterate and support a Post-it that's already on the board!)

Once you've completed this first category, have your notetaker write down the list of strengths and then move on to Weaknesses.

### Weaknesses

The process here is the same as with Strengths. Using the orange Post-its, give the team 15 minutes to jot down as many ideas as possible. This time, use the following prompts: What is holding us back? What is preventing us from achieving our long-term goals? What marketing skills are under-developed? Do we have processes that are inefficient? What are the issues, systems, or people that make it difficult for us to excel in everything we do?[14]

It's logical to pivot from what makes us strong to what makes us weak. These traits are interrelated. And they will change year-over-year. The goal is that once you identify a weakness you can work together to address it. Ideally, what was a weakness last year will have become a strength the next time you revisit your SWTO.

---

[14] It's absolutely critical that you have a conversation about your relationships with technical staff. The reality is that our firms are made up of human beings—all sorts of folks with different backgrounds, communication styles, time management abilities, and personality traits. We work in an industry wholly reliant on teamwork. If there are technical staff who are just plain hard to work with, you need to discuss it and discuss why. Making time for this allows marketing staff a safe space to vent, but more importantly, it creates an opportunity to devise ways to address and manage negative staff impacts on our time.

As with Strengths, the facilitator will begin sorting the Post-its and discuss with the group the common themes that emerge. Your notetaker will capture these and then you will move on to Threats.

## ▇ Threats

Using the same method as before, this time center your team around the barriers to improvements. Ask the following questions: "What prevents us from achieving our goals? What current systems, processes, or people hinder our ability to effectively manage our time? What is going on in the industry that worries us? What economic factors could negatively impact our firm?

The goal of the Threats analysis is different than Strengths or Weaknesses—many of the items that will make it up onto the board will be factors beyond our control—a weak economy, a firm owner who doesn't value the marketing staff, mismanagement of funding or staff resources. The point of this exercise is not to find solutions to all of these threats, but to acknowledge them. We have to collectively be aware of the forces at work against us. We may not be able to change them, but we can devise ways to respond to them, work around them, or in some cases neutralize them. Having the red flags present and accounted for allows the team to craft a strategy that is nimble and responsive to threats that lurk—either above or below the surface.

## ▇ Opportunities

Rounding out your SWTO analysis, take a moment with your team to review all of the topics presented in the last three exercises. Look at your Strengths, Weaknesses, and Threats in concert with each other. Many of your opportunities will be unlocked and discovered simply by reviewing each topic and flipping it over. If you listed an exceptionally strong relationship with a technical staffer as a strength, there is an opportunity to enlist that person as a vocal advocate for your marketing team. If you listed the underdevelopment of a service area as a weakness, you have an opportunity to devise ways to enhance and strengthen it. If you identified a softening of private-sector work as a threat, you have an opportunity to research and support business development in service areas that have steadier funding streams.

Often, this board typically has less Post-its than the others. Your team may be running out of energy due to the time the SWTO analysis takes, or it may simply be a lack of imagination. Focus your team's creative energy by pointing to the 'loudest' strengths, weaknesses, and threats and challenge them into thinking about how to harness those for the good of the team and the company. What ultimately lands on your Opportunities board will serve as the foundation for next year's priorities list.

---

### How to Retreat When You're a Team of One

When you're flying solo, it can be even more challenging to figure out how to prioritize and balance the competing demands of your job. If you are your firm's sole marketer, taking a day or half-day to get your bearings is a useful exercise. Follow the steps outlined in this chapter: review where your time has been going; plot out your calendar with your estimated proposal peaks, special projects, and personal milestones; and conduct your own SWTO analysis going through each one individually, then review your thoughts as a whole. Use this time to clinically assess where you are excelling and where you are struggling. Once you've completed your assessment and captured your priorities on your calendar, take a step back and think through what you will need to accomplish these priorities. Outline a set of bullets of your key takeaways. If you find yourself struggling to figure out how you can succeed in delivering on all of your objectives, consider your firm's willingness to engage an intern. If after your day of reflection you conclude that an extra hand would be beneficial to the firm, your bullet points and calendar will serve as the basis for a candid conversation with your boss.

## Building Out Your New Annual Priorities List

Now that you've worked your way through conversations around staff time and the SWTO analysis, it's time to revisit your wall calendar. Look at your Opportunities list with a critical eye and start envisioning how you will go about taking advantage of them. If you've identified the need to re-imagine your proposal process, think about the steps that would need to be taken to achieve that. If you've determined that your firm needs a style guide or new branding components, mentally walk through the set of activities you will need to implement such a project. If you know that your website is holding you back, determine if there is adequate time and resources to take that on in the coming year.

Ballpark the level of effort each opportunity would take. Ask yourselves, 'Is this a *want* to have or a *need* to have?' and prioritize your list starting with the needs. Once you've created that list, you can look at it in the context of your annual calendar and make judgment calls. "Can we really achieve all of these goals in the coming year? If not, what do we work on first?" Think in terms of a three-year plan. If you simply do not have time to address your full list, assign goals by Year 1, 2, and 3. You may find that many of your goals are interrelated and that one cannot happen until something else happens first. If you ended up with 9 major goals, perhaps you tackle three of them in the year to come, then earmark three for the next year and so on.

Once you determine as a team what special projects you can reasonably take on in the next year, you can begin assigning champions. This will directly tie back to those early conversations about staff time. Who has availability and at what time of year? Who is interested and passionate about the work? Ideally, you will find people raising their hands for certain projects. Work hard during this conversation to inspire excitement for the work ahead. It is much easier going into a new project with enthusiasm rather than dragging people along with you.

Once you have determined who will champion each effort, decide when the work will occur on your calendar. Break out the markers and capture these projects on the timeline. None of this is set it stone, but it will give you benchmarks to guide your planning efforts.

At this point, don't start diving down rabbit holes. This isn't the time to dig into the details about implementation plans. But this *is* the time to start setting meetings for kickoffs for each of your efforts. You may decide to do these kickoffs as part of your regular marketing check-ins or in one-on-ones between the champions and your Marketing Director. However you decide to tackle it, get the meetings scheduled during your retreat. Then take a breath, sit back and know that you have just walked through an enormous amount of great conversation and collaborative thinking.

A great way to wrap up your retreat is to re-center yourself in gratitude. Instead of focusing this inward, think beyond the people in the room. Discuss the technical staff who have been especially wonderful to work with. You may have mentioned them in your Strengths analysis. These are the champions and advocates of your team. The ones that always make time to say thank you, that you get materials on deadline, that make room for your voice and perspective in meetings. Now is the time to break out your small stack of thank-you cards. Take 15 minutes or so at the end of your meeting to quietly fill these out at a group. Have each person start by writing a thank-you card to a different staffer, then pass them around so that everyone on the team has a chance to add their remarks. When done, put them in envelopes. These might be mailed or simply left of their desks. This simple act of kindness further cements these positive relationships and will encourage your advocates to be even more vocal in their support of your marketing department.

Once the stack is done, take a breath, take pictures of all the wall notes, save your electronic notes, clean up your space, and thank each other. Go into your weekend knowing that you have just raised the bar for your team.

When you gather again the following week, don't just dive right back into deadlines. Make time at your check-in to recount the major takeaways and discuss what items you would like to share with your firm leadership. Your point person for communications will be tasked with carrying that message to them. After that has been relayed, you're ready to get to work on implementing on all of the great ideas you generated as a team.

**Retreat Essentials**

▶ Secure an off-site location. Rent a room at the library, borrow conference space at a teaming partner's office, or meet at one of your houses or apartments. Make sure your location has plenty of wall space. (You're going to need it!)

▶ Brainstorm your agenda each week for one month prior—let everyone have a say.

▶ Share your agenda with your firm's leadership and promise them a full report on your outcomes.

▶ Gather your materials: poster-sized Post-it paper, 3x3 inch Post-its, note pads, markers, sharpies, pens, easels (optional), and a stack of thank you cards.

▶ Set your out-of-office email, bring plenty of food, beverages, and energy. Turn off your phones or, better yet, don't bring them!

# CAUGHT IN THE UNDERTOW:
## WHAT COMES AFTER A LAYOFF

*"Losing a job is always rough. It knocks the wind out of your sails, but for me, it helped me realize that I was capable of much more than what was being asked of me at my last firm."*
Christopher T. (Marketing and Business Development Manager, engineering firm)

In a recession, sometimes—despite our best efforts—our firms make the call to lay off marketing staff. This can happen for a number of reasons—the firm is over-leveraged to the point of insolvency and must downsize across all departments or it merges with another firm and has to consolidate marketing resources. Sometimes the layoffs seem short-sighted, with cuts disproportionately affecting overhead positions. Whatever the motivation, when a layoff happens it is a jarring, frightening experience.

We go from a day-to-day world of fine-tuning technical staff resumes to fine-tuning our own. We may feel dejected. We may question our value, our talents, and our worth. "If my firm didn't want me, will anyone?" These feelings are natural. You are human. A layoff feels like a rejection and it hurts. Give yourself a break to feel that and acknowledge it, but don't get carried away.

Your *are* valuable. You *are* talented. You *are* worthy of your marketing title. And you are fortunate that you live during a time in human history where the idea of community has never been stronger in the job world. Your network, a solid understanding that the recession *will* pass, and your own ingenuity will see you through this.

CHAPTER NINETEEN

# LOOKING OUT AT THE HORIZON

"I had a good friend who called me the day I was laid off and said, 'Look, I know you. You're going to go to the gym and sweat it out, go home and eat a healthy dinner, and think you'll be fine. But you're going to wake up at 2 a.m. and panic. When you do, call me.' And that's exactly what happened. I woke up scared, mind racing, worrying about how I was going to pay my mortgage, second-guessing myself. I was filled with self-doubt."

Frank L. (Marketing and Strategy consultant)

A layoff may come with an abundance of remorse or happen in a quick and callous manner. Regardless of how the message is delivered, it hurts. And it thrusts you into an uncertain future. As discussed in Chapter 3, the average recession last 11 months. During this time, there will likely be more marketing professionals vying for less job openings. But be that as it may, the opportunities still abound. The beauty of marketing within the A/E/C industry is that our skills are transferable. For example, while you may have started your career at an architecture firm, making the leap to an engineering firm isn't difficult. Procurement processes are similar across our industries and the overlap in our networks and teaming partners create bridges between the service sectors.

It's also worth noting that there are A/E/C firms in virtually every large and mid-size city throughout the country. If you've been considering relocating, now is a perfect time to explore that. The Society for Marketing Professional Services (SMPS) has 58 chapters throughout the country that provide educational and career resources, including current job openings. And since each chapter is run by volunteers who work in the industry, by simply visiting a chapter's website you will find the names and contact information for a host of great marketing professionals. Start by reaching out for informational meetings. This is the time to expand your network and lean on each other for support.

> "I flew out for a week to do informational interviews. I reached out to the local chapter president of SMPS and had coffee and reached out to everyone I could think of that may have had connections in my new town. Everyone pitched in and was super helpful in putting me in touch with people. Even after I returned home, people would reach out saying things like, 'Hey, I heard this place is hiring'." – Lindsay D. (Marketing Manager, architecture firm)

It is also worth noting that our overall sense of community has evolved. This is our first recession in a 'smart phone' world. Coincidentally, the iPhone was released in 2007—right before the beginning of the Great Recession. Since then, the smart phone has drastically shaped and altered our personal and professional lives. This new paradigm of social connectivity has created a sense of community that simply didn't exist in the last recession. We have embraced 'self care'. We have grown and nurtured online communities that provide guidance and moral support. We have harnessed these connections to grow business during the expansion and we will now lean on them as we navigate our way through the recession.

Our 'emotional IQs' have never been higher. Couple that with the powerful force of networking via SMPS and the end result of this recession will no doubt be a stronger, more informed, and more vibrant community of marketing professionals.

### A Note on Freelance Work

Many marketers interviewed for this book mentioned the value in seeking freelance marketing work when in between jobs. This can take the form of out-sourced proposal coordination, editorial and design work, or strategy consultation. The key to success in securing freelance gigs is to find the nexus between your strongest skills and your strongest passions. Just because a firm downsizes its marketing resources doesn't mean the work disappears. By marketing yourself in the same ways you marketed your last firm, you can create an income stream and maintain your skills until you find your next full-time position.

"I have noticed that there are a lot more opportunities for remote positions at firms outside of your geography which bodes well for those of us that may need to job hunt soon."
Katherine P. (Director of Marketing, management consulting firm)

## Proposal Coordination

If anything, many firms will find themselves shorthanded when proposals pick up. This is an excellent time to pull out your list of contacts and let firms know that you are available to help with surplus proposals. When you find a firm that is interested and have negotiated a bill rate, initial meetings should take place to learn about internal systems, where to pull quals, access to templates, and to learn about their unique proposal process. Successful communication and a beautiful proposal will lay the groundwork for future requests.

## Editorial Work

A/E/C firms churn out an astonishing volume of text in the form of proposals, reports, and other content. Editorial QA/QC often falls to in-house marketing staff—who are often hard pressed for time in the best of circumstances, let alone when understaffed. This is an excellent opportunity to market yourself as an external resource. Editorial work requires little in terms of preparation other than understanding a firm's style guide. Once you have produced a few quality edits, you will likely find a repeat customer and a nice stream of side income.

## Design Work

As more and more firms embrace design software like the Adobe Creative Suite, the need for graphic design services continues to grow. A proficiency in InDesign alone can open up opportunities for freelance work, including report and proposal layout, cut-sheets, and other design elements. If this in an area of interest for you, having a handful of design examples on hand is usually all you need to start a conversation with firms who find themselves with a surplus of design work.

## Strategy Consultation

Have your greatest moments on the job taken place in the 'situation room'? Do you thrive on the thrill of orchestrating an interview team? Have you discovered the secret sauce for digital marketing campaigns and online brand development? Do you enjoy the thrill of brand introduction into new geographies? These are all highly orchestrated, strategic efforts that are well-suited for an external contractor who has the time, energy, and skills to tackle them without the pressing day-to-day deadlines of in-house staff. Securing this type of freelance marketing work takes more effort on the front-end, but given that you thrive on communication and brand enhancement, that shouldn't be too intimidating! You will need examples of how you've executed on similar work and glowing testimonials. Designing a simple website would be a valuable use of your time, as would engaging with your local chapter of SMPS to make connections and market your services.

"One of the things that's different this time around is that there are a lot of independent marketing consultants that have created a network where they share work. And they are located all over the country. They all have their own style of how they provide services, who they provide them to, and they have solid footing. If a time comes when companies decide they can't afford all of their in-house staff, I think these consultants will see a huge increase in work." – Bonnie T. (Strategic Pursuit Manager, environmental/water engineering firm)

### When Freelancing Becomes a Calling

For most, taking on side work is a great way to make ends meet while job-hunting. For some, it awakens in them an entrepreneurial spirit and drive. What starts as a stop-gap measure to bring in income becomes a calling. There are many marketing consulting firms that exist today because of past recessions and market volatility. And it makes sense. Marketers who prove to themselves (and others) that their skills are valuable on the open market often find that they have more fun working with multiple clients. It allows them the chance to use their palette of skills and ideas in different scenarios at different scales. This kind of diversity of environment is appealing to many as it keeps our skills sharp and provides ample room to learn and innovate.

Some of these marketing consultancies—once past the incubation stage—solidify into bonafide business ventures with enough work to warrant bringing on employees and investing in brand identity. This is a powerfully emotional and triumphant moment in any business owner's life. It is also an example of how dynamic and fertile the professional services industry can be—with new consulting firms emerging from the destructive environment of a recession.

"On a personal level, having gone through the Great Recession, I'm less concerned about the 'unknown'. A job is important, but I know I can weather the storm; my family can weather the storm. I've been there. You come through the other side one way or the other."
Craig R. (Marketing Manager, architecture firm)

Whether you freelance as a temporary measure or dive into something more entrepreneurial, the simple act of putting yourself out on the open market will teach you valuable lessons about courage, overcoming insecurities, and self-worth. Above all, lean on your connections with other marketing professionals. As the words of support and information-sharing on social media have shown us, this is a tight-knit band of people who are deeply interested in helping others. Embrace that.

Last, but not least, just breathe. You will get through this. You chose to dedicate your career to marketing because at heart you are a communicator. You are in tune with the world and you value social connections and community-building. You have a valuable place in this world and in this industry and you will land on your feet. Put your marketing skills to work and amplify You.

And remember, there are thousands of A/E/C firms throughout the country and the average recession lasts only 11 months. Watch the SMPS job boards, grow and nurture your network, market yourself on your social media feeds, and keep your eyes and ears open. The jobs will come.

"What would I tell my younger self? I would say, 'You can do anything. There is no limit to what you can do. You have the time and the brainpower to figure it out.' I was in such a panic that impostor syndrome took over in a big way for the first month. I didn't even know that was a thing. And it crushed me. If I could go back, I would say 'You are in the depths of impostor syndrome. You are a hard worker. You didn't get a far as you've come by chance. You can do anything. Recognize your gifts, recognize your strengths, and realize what you can do with those strengths.' – Frank L. (Marketing and Strategy consultant)

## ABOUT THE AUTHOR

 Allison Tivnon joined the A/E/C industry in 2008. She has dedicated her career to city and regional planning—partnering with Cities, Counties, regional governments, DOTs, and others on behalf of urban planners, transportation engineers, economists, and policy analysts. She started her career as a proposal coordinator and worked her way up to Marketing Director and Partner.

*Marketing at Low Tide:*
*How to Recession-Proof Your Marketing Department*
began as a presentation that Allison has given at events, conferences, and in webinars for the Society of Marketing Professional Services (SMPS) and the American Council of Engineering Companies (ACEC).

In 2019, she was awarded the Influential Marketing Leader of the Year award by the Oregon chapter of SMPS.

In May 2020, Allison was elected to the Beaverton City Council in Oregon. She will take office on January 1, 2021.

**Connect with Allison on LinkedIn:**

https://www.linkedin.com/in/allison-tivnon-04453661/

CPSIA information can be obtained
at www.ICGtesting.com
Printed in the USA
JSHW010742040521
14283JS00009B/28

9 781735 743707